THE
RISE
OF THE

NONES

UNDERSTANDING AND REACHING
THE RELIGIOUSLY UNAFFILIATED

JAMES EMERY WHITE

BakerBooks

a division of Baker Publishing Group
Grand Rapids, Michigan

© 2014 by James Emery White

Published by Baker Books
a division of Baker Publishing Group
P.O. Box 6287, Grand Rapids, MI 49516-6287
www.bakerbooks.com

Printed in the United States of America

Library of Congress Cataloging-in-Publication Data is on file at the Library of Congress, Washington, DC.

ISBN 978-0-8010-1623-3

Unless otherwise indicated, Scripture quotations are from the Holy Bible, New International Version®. NIV®. Copyright © 1973, 1978, 1984, 2011 by Biblica, Inc.™ Used by permission of Zondervan. All rights reserved worldwide. www.zondervan.com

Scripture quotations labeled Message are from *The Message* by Eugene H. Peterson, copyright © 1993, 1994, 1995, 2000, 2001, 2002. Used by permission of NavPress Publishing Group. All rights reserved.

Scripture quotations labeled NLT are from the *Holy Bible*, New Living Translation, copyright © 1996, 2004, 2007 by Tyndale House Foundation. Used by permission of Tyndale House Publishers, Inc., Carol Stream, Illinois 60188. All rights reserved.

Scripture quotations labeled Phillips are from The New Testament in Modern English, revised edition—J. B. Phillips, translator. © J. B. Phillips 1958, 1960, 1972. Used by permission of Macmillan Publishing Co., Inc.

Scripture quotations labeled TLB are from *The Living Bible*, copyright © 1971. Used by permission of Tyndale House Publishers, Inc., Wheaton, Illinois 60189. All rights reserved.

Material taken from *Christ Among the Dragons*, copyright © 2010 by James Emery White, is used by permission of InterVarsity Press, P.O. Box 1400, Downers Grove, IL 60515, www.ivpress.com.

14 15 16 17 18 19 20   7 6 5 4 3 2

Contents

12. Opening the Front Door   151
13. Reimagining the Church   165

    Afterword   179
    Appendix A: Judged   183
    Appendix B: The Spirituality Grid   195
    Notes   209

Acknowledgments

I wish to thank the Baker team for their support of this project, our fifth together, and specifically Robert Hosack who has now bravely edited three.

The gracious help of Grayson Pope and Keith Main on the final manuscript was, well, gracious. Glynn Goble keeps my life ordered so that I can write; Alli Main orders her life in a way to help me write and selflessly serves my writing process in a way that cannot be lauded enough; and my wife, Susan, continues to make every page possible.

Finally, my thanks goes to Mecklenburg Community Church, an amazing community of people who die to themselves daily in countless ways in order to reach out to their friends and family, neighbors, and co-workers with the message of Christ. It's an honor to be your pastor.

Introduction

This is a book on the rise of the *"nones,"* now the fastest-growing religious group in America. These religiously unaffiliated people have always been with us, of course, but their new classification and the vast numbers who have flocked to their nonlabel label in just a few short years have been breathtaking.

This book is divided into two parts. The first part is an analysis of the rise of the *nones*, with a look at the rise itself, the characteristics of the average *none*, why the *nones* are on the rise, the broader cultural context of our post-Christian world and its relationship to the rise, and the various beliefs present among the religiously unaffiliated. In short, the first section will give you the cultural analysis needed to understand the who, what, and why of the rise of the *nones*.

I write not simply as a professor of theology and culture who is attempting to investigate a new cultural phenomenon, but also as a pastor; so this discussion is far from academic. For the last two decades I have led a church that targets the religiously unaffiliated in all of its outreach. To date, over 70 percent of our total growth has come from the previously unchurched. I know that is a staggeringly high number, but it has been the dynamic of our church from its inception. So I write not only as one who has been reaching out to the *nones* for over twenty years, but also as one who has seen firsthand how that outreach is now having to change.

That brings me to the second part of the book, which is an overview of the new mentality and approach that is needed to connect with the rising tide of the religiously unaffiliated and not only reach them for Christ, but also involve them in the life of the church. But do not expect a list of tips and techniques; what is called for is nothing less than a revolution of mindset and strategy.

Finally, I've provided two appendices that feature two talks delivered at Mecklenburg Community Church (Meck). One of the most frequent questions following conferences and seminars is, "Okay, I get this. So how do you actually talk to a *none*? What would a sermon attempting to reach out to them sound like and feel like?" The two talks are indicative of how one could address some of the key concerns present among the *nones*.

The two parts of this book remind me of something I once read about the late Francis Schaeffer. Someone questioned him about his engagement of culture in relation to apologetics, asking whether he was an evidentialist or a presuppositionalist.

Schaeffer thought a moment and said, "Actually, I think I'm just an old-fashioned evangelist." And that is what, in the end, I am. And what I hope, in the end, this book affords others to be as well.

☑ PART 1

1

The Rise of the *Nones*

A recent issue of *Foreign Policy* magazine was focused around its first-ever set of predictions about the future. Articles from some of the world's most "bleeding-edge" thinkers looked ahead at the planet in the year 2025.

As you can imagine, most of their predictions have already been set in motion by recent events and could easily have been predicted. For example, technology will take on a life of its own; micromultinationals will run the world; everything will be too big to fail; the South China Sea will be the future of conflict; the world will be more crowded (but with older people); the shape of the global economy will fundamentally change; and problems will be increasingly global in nature, as will their solutions.

What intrigued me the most, however, was a submission titled "Megatrends That Weren't."[1] Joshua Keating took a careful look at "Yesterday's Next Big Things" that have yet to take place, concluding that "history can be awfully unkind to pundits wielding crystal balls." As his examples show, today's "Next Big Thing" can quickly become tomorrow's "Trend That Never Was." For example:

The Japanese Superpower. In the 1980s and early '90s, as Japan's industrial production surged by more than 50 percent, a cottage industry predicting Japan's economic dominance was born. Instead, Japan entered its *lost decade* of economic stagnation and was overtaken by China in 2010.

The Permanent Economic Boom. Prior to the current financial crisis, there was unbridled optimism that the good times don't have to end. Experts placed inordinate faith in the power of computerized trading, financial innovation, and the exploding housing market. The reality is that even by 2013, the Dow Jones Industrial Average has never faired significantly better than its then 2007 peak of 14,164.53. So much for predictions of the Dow reaching 36,000, 40,000, or even 100,000, as some predicted.

Peak Oil. While there is a finite amount of oil in the world and it's going to run out sooner or later, it was predicted that global oil production would tap out in the early 1970s. Peak-oil theorists failed to take into account both the discovery of new oil and new means of extracting difficult-to-recover reserves buried deep beneath the ocean or in tar sands in the Canadian tundra.

The Resource Crunch. In 1798, English scholar Thomas Malthus predicted that global famine and disease would eventually limit human population growth. As of the time of this writing, we are now more than 7 billion and growing without imminent global famine and catastrophe due to rapid population growth. There may come a time when the earth's population becomes unsustainable, but for now the problem isn't a lack of resources but how to distribute them to those in need.

The Internet Fad. Excessive skepticism can be as bad as buying into overly optimistic predictions. In 1943 IBM Chairman Thomas Watson saw a global market for "maybe five computers." Then there's astronomer and popular science author Clifford Stoll, who in a 1995 book and *Newsweek* article ridiculed the idea that "we'll soon buy books and newspapers straight over the Internet" and argued that "no online database will replace your daily newspaper." And more recently, British entrepreneur Alan Sugar predicted in 2005 that the iPod would be "kaput" within the year.

But there is one prediction that recently has been supported with multiple stunning confirmations that few dispute: the future religious landscape of America will be increasingly dominated by the *nones*.

The ARIS Shock

The first indication of this new reality was evidenced by the headlines surrounding the results of the 2008 American Religious Identification Survey (ARIS):[2]

> "Almost All Denominations Losing Ground: Faith Is Shifting, Drifting or Vanishing Outright" (*USA Today*)[3]
>
> "We're Losing Our Religion" (Associated Press)[4]
>
> "America Becoming Less Christian" (CNN.com)[5]
>
> "US Religion ID Inching to 'None'" (*Seattle Times*)[6]
>
> "None of Thee Above" (Religion News Service)[7]

Much in the study was to be expected: mainlines are losing ground; the Bible Belt is less Baptist; Catholics have invaded the South; denominationalism is on the wane. What generated the headlines was the increase in a category few had previously discussed: the *nones*.

What are the *nones*? The short answer is that they are the religiously unaffiliated. When asked about their religion, they did not answer "Baptist" or "Catholic" or any other defined faith. They picked a new category: *none*.

Percentage of Americans Claiming No Religious Identity

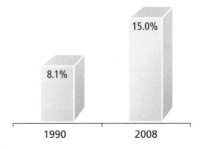

The ARIS survey found that the *nones* nearly doubled from a 1990 survey to 2008, from 8.1 percent to 15 percent, making those who claimed no religion at all the third-largest defined constituency in the United States. Only Catholics and Baptists represented larger groups. Further, *nones* were the only religious bloc to rise in percentage in every single state, thus constituting the only true national religious trend. The official ARIS report, titled "American Nones: The Profile of the No Religion Population," found that the 1990s was the decade when the "secular boom" occurred. During that era alone, each year 1.3 million more adult Americans joined the ranks of the *nones*.[8]

But the *nones* weren't done booming.

Souls in Transition

The next confirmation that a sea change was underway came when Trinity College in Hartford, Connecticut, released another slice of ARIS findings.[9] It is important to note that findings from ARIS have, by necessity, come in doses. Done in 1990 with more than 113,000 people, again in 2001, and then again in 2008 with more than 54,000 people, it was one of the largest demographic polls in history and perhaps the largest survey of American religions to date.

The headline? Gen Xers, as they age, are bucking all conventional wisdom and not returning to the religious fold. This was newsworthy because of the long-held view that young people raised in the church may sow a few wild oats, drift away from the compulsory attendance inflicted by their parents, but then return once they marry and begin having children. That's the way it worked with baby boomers—after all, Woodstock alums had led to the development of Willow Creek, then the largest church in North America. So there was little concern when Millennials left the church in droves once they became independent from their parents.

But that isn't what is happening. "The ARIS study seems to challenge what has been a core truth of American demographics: That people become more politically conservative and religiously affiliated as they age. . . . Everything we find here is counterintuitive," reflects Barry Kosmin, an author of the study.[10]

This new reality of the "young and unchurched" becoming the "older and unchurched" is in line with the results from the National Study of Youth and Religion, initially conducted from 2001 to 2005 and arguably the largest research project on the religious and spiritual lives of American adolescents. The first round of results was analyzed in a groundbreaking work titled *Soul Searching: The Religious and Spiritual Lives of Teenagers*. When they were no longer teenagers but "emerging adults" between the ages of eighteen and twenty-three, a new release of results—titled *Souls in Transition: The Religious and Spiritual Lives of Emerging Adults*—revealed the findings of the study as it entered its next phase.[11] (Note that the word *emerging* here has nothing to do with the emergent church or emergent movement; instead it refers to their relationship with adulthood—they are making their way into adulthood in a stretched-out, prolonged manner.) Among these emerging adults are six major religious types:

1. committed traditionalists (no more than 15 percent)
2. selective adherents (perhaps 30 percent)
3. spiritually open (about 15 percent)
4. religiously indifferent (at least 25 percent)
5. religiously disconnected (no more than 5 percent)
6. irreligious (no more than 10 percent)

While only 15 percent would be committed to any type of religious faith, 25 percent are indifferent, another 5 percent disconnected, and another 10 percent completely irreligious. That's 40 percent of all emerging adults clearly distanced from religion.

The largest group, the religiously indifferent, "neither care to practice religion nor to oppose it. They are simply not invested in religion either way."[12] If they had a motto, it would be: "It just doesn't matter that much." To them, "religion has a status on the relevance structures or priority lists . . . similar to . . . the oil refinery industry."[13] Yet indifference was not relegated to this group. In truth, indifference permeated all of the categories in one form or another.

The Rise of the *Nones*

The rise of the *nones* did not get our full attention until the Pew Forum on Religion and Public Life weighed in with their most recent study. Titled "Nones on the Rise," the study found that one in five Americans (19.3 percent) now claim no religious identity.

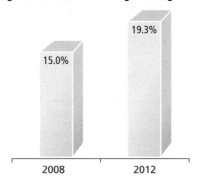

Percentage of Americans Claiming No Religious Identity

Among the unaffiliated are more than 13 million self-described atheists and agnostics, which is nearly 6 percent of the U.S. public, as well as nearly 33 million people who say they have no particular religious affiliation (14 percent).[14] This puts the United States in close proximity to the U.K., where the *nones* constitute 25 percent of the population.[15] The Pew study also found that Protestant Christianity no longer constitutes the majority in the United States, declining from 53 percent to 48 percent since 2007 alone. For perspective, it was as high as two out of every three Americans in the 1960s. These findings were later supported by a team of sociologists from the University of California, Berkeley, and Duke University who analyzed data on religious attitudes as part of the General Social Survey, a highly cited annual poll conducted by an independent research institute at the University of Chicago.[16]

To put this in perspective, consider that the number of *nones* in the 1930s and '40s hovered around 5 percent. By 1990 that number had only risen to 8 percent, a mere 3 percent rise in over half a century.[17] Between 1990 and 2008—just eighteen years—the number of *nones* leaped from 8.1 percent to 15 percent. Then, in just four short years, it climbed to 20 percent, representing one of every five Americans. Even more telling was the discovery in the National Study of Youth and Religion that a third of U.S. adults under the age of thirty don't identify with a religion.

Percentage of Americans Claiming No Religious Identity

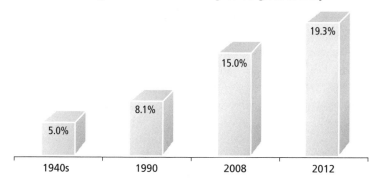

| 1940s | 1990 | 2008 | 2012 |

5.0% 8.1% 15.0% 19.3%

So where have the *nones* gone? Nowhere. There is no shift from Protestant Christianity to another religious brand. Instead, there is simply the abandonment of a defined religion altogether. Those who previously were simply "unchurched," or who had infrequent attendance, are now dropping religious attachments completely. Given the choice to label themselves as "nothing" instead of "something," they prefer "nothing."

The *nones* now make up the nation's fastest-growing and second-largest religious category, eclipsed only by Catholics, outnumbering even Southern Baptists, the largest Protestant denomination.

Should We Be That Concerned?

To be sure, there are those who say this is nothing to be overly alarmed about. Some, such as church growth consultant Charles Arn, dismiss it as being little more than a rejection of institutional affiliation, and that nearly every membership-based organization is losing members. As a result, it's not a spiritual issue at all.

Others, such as sociologist Christian Smith, leader of the National Study of Youth and Religion, agree it's not quite a "sea change from seriously religious to unbelieving," yet still see it as a "longer-term distancing of some from any association with religious faith and practice, which is significant." While arguing from similar Gallup polls for a slightly slower rise among the unaffiliated than the Pew findings indicate, Frank Newport from Gallup still calls it an "important shift"— but most do not hedge their bets.

"This is a big story," says Clyde Wilcox, professor at Georgetown University. David Kinnaman, president of the Barna Group, says, "This is a major trend in American religion."[18] Dan Gilgoff, outgoing Religion Editor at CNN, makes the following assertion as he reflects on his tenure: "The explosion of people with no religion will be a huge story in this century, and the news media have only begun to explore its many implications." He says the press has yet to dig into "countless other stories about making meaning, tradition, and ethics in a post-religious existence."[19]

One dynamic that clearly tempers the results is that this trend is only an American phenomenon, not a global one. After a century-long decline, global religious affiliation is now on the rise, with Africa and China experiencing the most dramatic religious change. According to Todd Johnson, director of the Center for the Study of Global Christianity, globally only 12 percent claimed no religious affiliation in 2010, compared to 20 percent in 1970. But this growth is coming from the south, not the north. Christians in the Global North comprised 80 percent of all Christians in 1920 but today make up less than 40 percent. In Africa alone, Christian affiliation has risen from 9 percent to 47.9 percent over the last one hundred years.[20]

The United States, however, is in the Global North—a region that is increasingly made up of people like twenty-eight-year-old Claire Noelle Frost, who told *USA Today* she was once a Christian until she "let go of belief. . . . There's so much I cannot prove. I'm not sure truth exists at all. Instead of 'I believe,' I say 'maybe,' and 'who knows?'"[21]

So who are these *nones*? Not who you may think.

Questions for Discussion and Reflection

1. When you read that "the future religious landscape of America will be increasingly dominated by the *nones*," were you surprised?

2. The 2008 ARIS study that first charted the rise of the *nones* from 1990 to 2008 found that the *nones* had nearly doubled from 8.1 to 15 percent. That made those who claim no religious affiliation the third-largest defined religious constituency in the United States. Based on your own life experience and the community around you, does that seem accurate?

3. An important insight learned about Gen Xers is that as they age, they are not returning to religion as originally assumed. Have you seen this in your own church? What does this mean for you as a church leader or member?

4. One of the biggest challenges for churches today is the 40 percent of all emerging adults who are clearly distanced from religion. What is your church doing right now to reach the *nones*? What is your church doing that may further distance them?

5. If the "religiously indifferent," those who neither care to practice nor oppose religion, had a motto, it would be: "It just doesn't matter that much." Do you see this reflected in society? Where and among whom?

6. Perhaps the largest shock related to the rise of the *nones* came from the Pew study titled "Nones on the Rise." This study found that one in five Americans (19.3 percent) now claim no religious identity. How does that statistic alter how you engage your community?

7. Throughout all of the studies you read about is an underlying current that *nones* are simply leaving religion altogether. They are not going from Protestant Christianity to something else; they are dropping off the map altogether. Can you think of some reasons why?

8. What was made apparent by all of the studies chronicling the rise of the *nones* is that the landscape of American Christianity has changed. Given that, have your methods changed along with it? How?

2

Snapshots

Now that we've documented the *nones* as the fastest-growing and now third-largest religious constituency in the United States—constituting one of every five Americans—who are they? Studies reveal that they are not made up of *seekers* who are looking for a spiritual home but simply haven't found it yet (more on that later). Nor are they products of a hostile college system intent on a secular indoctrination, real as that may be. Surveys show that religious affiliation is declining among Americans who do not have college degrees as well as among college graduates.

Here's the real snapshot of who a *none* is.[1]

1. *Male.* Though fewer than half of Americans are male, 56 percent of *nones* are male. The gender divide among *nones* who are atheists or agnostics is even more pronounced: 64 percent of this group is male.

2. *Young.* The older the American, the more likely he or she is to be affiliated with a religion. One-third of Americans under thirty say they have no religious affiliation, compared to 9 percent of those sixty-five and older. This is mostly due to "generational replacement" as a younger generation assumes the place of an older one that is decidedly more religious.

3. *White.* Of all *nones*, 71 percent are white, 11 percent are Hispanic, 9 percent are black, and 4 percent are Asian. If you narrow the pool to just agnostics and atheists, the group is even whiter: 82 percent.

4. *Not necessarily an atheist.* The largest group of *nones* (68 percent) say they believe in God or a universal spirit. Within that group, 30 percent of them are certain God exists. Only 27 percent of *nones* say there is no God.

5. *Not very religious.* This may sound obvious, but it makes the distinction between a person who has no religious affiliation, and one who is not religious. There are some *nones* who do consider themselves religious—just outside the confines of a religious organization. Nearly three-quarters of *nones* (72 percent) seldom or never attend religious services.

6. *A Democrat. Nones* are among the most reliably Democratic of voters. In 2008, three-quarters of them voted for Barack Obama and 23 percent for John McCain, making them as strongly Democratic as white evangelicals were Republican. More than six in ten of those who are registered voters are Democrats or lean toward the Democratic Party.

7. *In favor of abortion and same-gender marriage being legal.* Big gaps separate *nones* and Americans in general on these issues. While 53 percent of the general public say abortion should be legal in all or most circumstances, 72 percent of the unaffiliated do. And while at the time of the study 48 percent of the general public favored same-sex marriage, 73 percent of *nones* did.

8. *Liberal or moderate*—and not just on the issues above. More than three-quarters of *nones* describe themselves as generally liberal or moderate, compared to the one in five who call themselves conservative.

9. *Not necessarily hostile toward religious institutions.* He or she just doesn't want to belong to one. More than half of the *nones* (52 percent) say religious institutions protect and strengthen morality, though an even greater proportion (70 percent) believe these institutions are too concerned with money and power.

10. *Most likely a westerner.* In the U.S., *nones* are most concentrated in the West and least concentrated in the South. While 23 percent of Americans live in the West, 30 percent of *nones* do.

A Portrait of a "None"

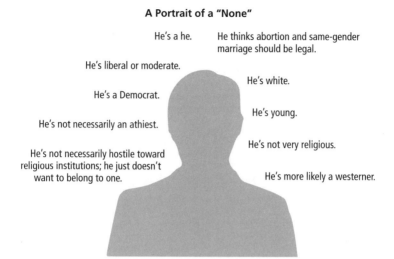

He's a he.

He thinks abortion and same-gender marriage should be legal.

He's liberal or moderate.

He's white.

He's a Democrat.

He's young.

He's not necessarily an athiest.

He's not very religious.

He's not necessarily hostile toward religious institutions; he just doesn't want to belong to one.

He's more likely a westerner.

Spiritual but Not Religious

What is most important to understand about the average *none* is that *most are not atheists*. In truth, most still believe in God, and many pray on a daily basis. They consider themselves spiritual, or at least open to spirituality.

The real mark of a *none* is not the rejection of God but the rejection of any specific religion. When it comes to content, dogma, orthodoxy—anything spelled out or offering a system of beliefs—they've gone from "I believe" to "Maybe" to "Who knows?" When pressed as to what they do hold to, they collectively answer, "Nothing in particular." Simply put, they are spiritual but not religious.

They may not want to say "I'm a Baptist," but that does not equate with "I don't believe in God." In other words, there is a strong reticence toward labels of any kind. It may help to visualize it in terms of a religious axis and a spiritual axis, creating four quadrants.

The caricature of a *none* places him or her in the "Not Religious, Not Spiritual" category—but that is inaccurate. The vast majority belong in the "Spiritual, Not Religious" quadrant.

Consider Marcus Mumford, the twenty-six-year-old lead singer of the phenomenally successful British band Mumford & Sons. Mumford

	Religious Not Spiritual	Religious Spiritual
RELIGIOUS	Not Religious Not Spiritual	Not Religious Spiritual

S P I R I T U A L

is the son of John and Eleanor Mumford, the national leaders of the Vineyard Church in the U.K. and Ireland, part of the international, evangelical Christian Vineyard Movement. He recently married actress Carey Mulligan, whom he'd met years earlier at a Christian youth camp. As the main lyricist for the band, he has lavished the music of Mumford & Sons with the themes and imagery of faith, often drawing specifically on the Christian tradition. As Cathleen Falsani has observed, they "explore relationships with God and others; fears and doubts; sin, redemption, and most of all, grace."[2]

Yet in a *Rolling Stone* interview, Mumford declined to claim the "Christian" label as his own. The reporter asked Mumford whether he "still consider[s] himself a Christian." Mumford replied:

> I don't really like that word. It comes with so much baggage. So, no, I wouldn't call myself a Christian. I think the word just conjures up all these religious images that I don't really like. I have my personal views about the person of Jesus and who he was. . . . I've kind of separated myself from the culture of Christianity.[3]

Describing his spiritual journey as a "work in progress," Mumford said that he's never doubted the existence of God and that his

parents are not bothered about his
ambivalence toward the Christian
label. Before anyone makes a rush
to judgment, Falsani suggests that
we "consider why he chose to answer the way he did."

She continues, "What I heard
in his reticence to label himself a
Christian was not a denial of faith,
but instead something that falls
between Dorothy Day's famous
'Don't call me a saint—I don't want
to be dismissed so easily,' and Søren
Kierkegaard's, 'Once you label me
you negate me.'"[4] She also hears echoes of another rock star whose
own Christian faith has been a topic of conversation. When Bono was
the same age Mumford is now, he shied away from Christian labels
and stopped talking about his faith in public forums. When asked
about his faith in a 1987 interview in *Rolling Stone*, Bono said, "I am
a Christian, but at times I feel very removed from Christianity. The
Jesus Christ that I believe in was the man who turned over the tables
in the temple and threw the money-changers out."[5] Fifteen years later,
in 2002, Bono told Falsani, "By the way, I don't set myself up to be
any kind of Christian. I can't live up to that. It's something I aspire
to, but I don't feel comfortable with that badge."[6]

Such statements by Mumford and Bono, and the legions of *nones*
like them, are not disavowals of faith or beliefs. Instead, they are the
rejection of a label related to faith or belief. In years past, an unchurched individual might still claim to be Baptist or Catholic; now
there is great cultural freedom to drop the label entirely. The speed at
which this has happened supports an old thesis of church historian
Martin Marty, who wrote a book half a century ago on varieties of
unbelief and who has long thought that religious cohesion "has long
been overstated."[7]

> **Three Groupings of the Religiously Unaffiliated**
>
> 1. Those who were raised totally outside of orga- nized religion
> 2. Those who became un- happy with their religion and left
> 3. Those who never really engaged with religion in the first place, even though they were raised in a religious household

This follows how John Green, a senior research adviser at Pew, breaks the religiously unaffiliated Americans into three groups:

1. Those who were raised totally outside of organized religion
2. Those who became unhappy with their religion and left
3. Those who never really engaged with religion in the first place, even though they were raised in a religious household

Green says, "In the past, we would describe those people as nominally affiliated. They might say, 'I am Catholic; I am a Baptist,' but they never went [to services]. Now, they feel a lot more comfortable just saying, 'You know, I am really nothing.'"[8]

No Longer Seekers

But it's more than simply being *nothing*. Perhaps one of the more disconcerting marks of typical *nones* is that they are very content with holding their "nothing in particular" stance toward religion. Among those who say they believe in "nothing in particular," 88 percent are not even looking for a specific faith or religion.

Think of their stance like this:

Spirituality? "Yes."

God? "Probably."

A specific religion? "Not for me."

But at least seeking? "No, not really. Not a priority."

The detrimental effect for a church or denomination could not be more complete. It is akin to having a world full of people being open and even interested in coffee, but purposefully driving past Starbucks with complete disinterest.

The significance of this cannot be overstated. For the last few decades, the key word in most conversations about evangelism and church growth has been the word *seeker*. As in "seeker churches," being "seeker-targeted" in strategy, and in talk about reaching "seekers," or what a "seeker" may think about our service. And let's not forget the widespread embrace of being "seeker-driven" and "seeker-sensitive."

All things "seeker" came onto the scene during the late seventies and were vibrant until the mid-nineties. It is now irrelevant at best and terribly misleading at worst. The term *seeker* was used to refer in a general way to the unchurched who were turned off to church but open to both spirituality and religion. Think back to the flood of baby boomers who wanted to find a church for their kids but felt freedom from the religious and denominational moorings of their youth. They weren't rejecting religion per se; they just felt the freedom to explore other traditions. For example, consider the number of Catholics who explored nondenominational, evangelical megachurches. These were people who were truly seeking, open to exploring the Christian faith for their life, and often in active search mode for a religious faith, and even home, in order to plant themselves. They had rejected the religion of their upbringing (often Catholicism), not religion itself.

As the ARIS report concludes, "The challenge to Christianity . . . does not come from other religions but from a rejection of all forms of organized religion."[9] Barry Kosmin, co-researcher for the survey, adds, "They're not thinking about religion and rejecting it; they're not thinking about it at all."[10] Or as the research of the Pew Forum on Religion and Public Life found, "The unaffiliated say they are not looking for a religion that would be right for them."[11]

So much for seeking.

Jonathan Rauch, in an article for the *Atlantic Monthly*, coined a term to describe his own spiritual condition. After a couple of glasses of Merlot, someone asked him about his religion. He was about to say "atheist" when it dawned on him that wasn't quite accurate. "I used to call myself an atheist," he finally responded, "and I still don't believe in God, but the larger truth is that it has been years since I really cared one way or another. I'm"—and this was when it hit him—"an . . . apatheist!" Rauch went on to describe his state as a "disinclination to care all that much about one's own religion, and an even stronger disinclination to care about other people's."[12]

He's not alone. According to the 2011 Baylor University Religion Survey, 44 percent said they spend no time seeking "eternal wisdom." And in a study by LifeWay Research, 46 percent said they never wonder whether they will go to heaven. So when it comes to matters related to

God, religion, or even atheism, millions simply shrug their shoulders and say, "So what?"[13]

A Land of Swedes

In his book *Society Without God*, sociologist Phil Zuckerman chronicles his fourteen months investigating Danes' and Swedes' feelings about religion. His conclusion? Religion "wasn't really so much a private, personal issue, but rather, a non-issue."[14] His interviewees just didn't care about it. As one replied, "I really have never thought about that. . . . It's been fun to get these kinds of questions that I never, never think about."[15] It brings to mind how sociologist Peter Berger once quipped, "If India is the most religious country on our planet, and Sweden is the least religious, America is a land of Indians ruled by Swedes."[16] What we must now realize is that we are increasingly becoming simply a land of Swedes.

But that does not mean they do not have an "unofficial" dogma. Because they do.

Questions for Discussion and Reflection

1. Nearly three-quarters of *nones* (72 percent) seldom or never attend a religious service. This means you cannot continue investing only in those who are already in your seats. Has the outreach strategy of your church changed, or how does it need to change, to reach those 72 percent of *nones*?

2. One of the biggest complaints *nones* have against organized religion is that it is too concerned with money and power. How can your church work to disprove their perception? Are you actively doing so already?

3. One of the most important things to understand about *nones* is that most of them are not atheists. Their defining characteristic is not the rejection of God but the rejection of a specific religion. They are spiritual but not religious. What does that mean for how they interpret the world and for how they view religion?

4. A glaring statistic that points to a specific change in missional strategy is that 88 percent of those who believe in "nothing in particular" are not actively looking for a specific faith or religion. Translation: they are not seekers. Much of our outreach strategy since the 1970s has been based on a seeker-driven America. How does your church's outreach strategy need to change based on the fact that those you are called to reach are not even looking for you?

5. One of the most thought-provoking quotes from the ARIS study is from Barry Kosmin. He says, "They're [the *nones*] not thinking about religion and rejecting it; they're not thinking about it at all." Does that correspond with your perception of the unchurched?

6. As noted earlier, when it comes to matters related to God or religion, millions simply shrug their shoulders and say, "So what?" How does that change how you interact with the unchurched in your community?

7. One thing *nones* reject is the thought of being labeled or being marked with any specific brand. Why do you think that is?

8. Were you surprised by the description of a typical *none* at the beginning of the chapter?

3

Lawyers, Guns, and Money

Have you ever heard the phrase, "the perfect storm"? The idea was first introduced through a book by Sebastian Junger, later made into a movie starring George Clooney, called *The Perfect Storm*.[1] It was based on a true event.

In October of 1991, the elements all came together to create the most powerful storm in recorded history. It struck just off the coast of Gloucester, Massachusetts. It was really three storms in one: a hurricane, energy flowing from the Great Lakes, and a frontal system sweeping through New England. It created an almost apocalyptic situation in the Atlantic, with boats encountering waves of one hundred feet, which is the equivalent of a ten-story building.

It was the National Weather Service that called it "the Perfect Storm." It took the lives of many people, including the six men aboard the swordfishing boat *Andrea Gail*, made famous through its Hollywood depiction.

Since then, whenever multiple dynamics come together to create an overwhelming impact, it is called a "perfect storm." When it comes to modern assaults on faith, there have been two such cataclysmic events. The first was the combination of the ideas of Copernicus, Darwin, and Freud.[2]

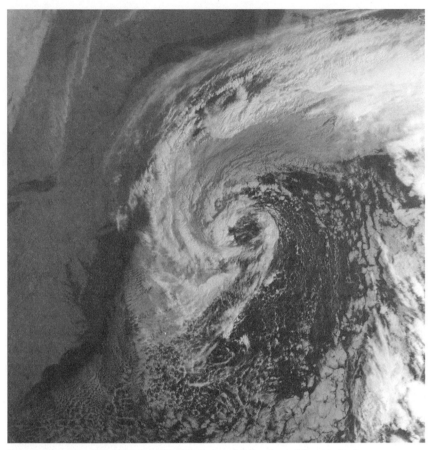

"The Perfect Storm," October 1991, US National Oceanic and Atmospheric Administration

Copernicus initiated what can be termed the *cosmological attack*. In determining through his telescope that we live in a heliocentric universe, as opposed to an Earth-centered one, he challenged more than the centrality of human existence on planet Earth; he brought into question the trustworthiness of faith itself.

At the time, the official teaching of the Christian church considered anything other than an Earth-centered universe heresy. Of course, the church's position was wrong. It wasn't that the Bible was wrong, only their interpretation of obscure texts that had been skewed by the bias that Earth needed to be at the center of creation to uphold the special nature of God's creation on Earth. No such assertion was necessary to the doctrine of creation, much less the doctrine of humanity, but the damage had been done. Religious pronouncements on matters of public discourse have been automatically suspect ever since, and modern cosmologists now speak to issues of faith and philosophy with greater authority than priests and theologians.

Darwin's assault was not cosmological; it was biological—or perhaps more accurately, anthropological. In *Origin of Species*, this minister's son contended that the origin of humankind could be accounted for in ways other than direct spiritual activity—namely, natural selection. No matter that the theory of macroevolution continues to have its fair share of detractors in regard to its failure to account for the actual origin of species (e.g., one of the pushbacks against naturalistic evolution is that you need self-reproducing organisms in place for natural selection to even begin), the very idea of an alternative explanation rooted in science proved compelling. And of course, few believers at the time considered the idea of theistic evolution.[3]

Modern Assaults on Faith: The first "perfect storm"

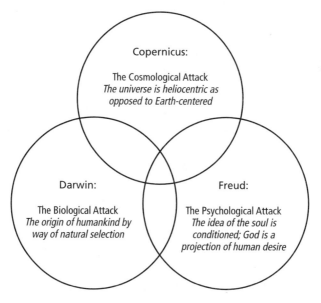

Copernicus:

The Cosmological Attack
The universe is heliocentric as opposed to Earth-centered

Darwin:

The Biological Attack
The origin of humankind by way of natural selection

Freud:

The Psychological Attack
The idea of the soul is conditioned; God is a projection of human desire

Nonetheless, the damage was done. Neither Earth nor human beings were pictured as the center of the universe.

Then Sigmund Freud used psychology to intimate that the idea of the soul itself is conditioned. God is nothing but a projection of our desires. We want there to be a God, so we imagine such a being. Or as Voltaire wrote in 1770, "*Se Dieu n'existait pas, il faudrait l'inventer*" ("If God did not exist, it would be necessary to invent him"). Forgetting that such an argument would war against the integrity of many of the intellectual achievements of civilization, including his own theory of psychoanalysis, Freud hit his target in the same manner as Darwin. There was now an option to explain spiritual conviction apart from faith but seemingly rooted in that which was intellectually apprehensible.

The first perfect storm was complete. But another was brewing, and it all started in the 1990s.

The Secular Boom

You remember the '90s, right? It was a patchwork quilt of events and ideas, movements and personalities if there ever was one. Our headlines changed and moved with the fast-pace nature of a video camera.

In August of 1990, Saddam Hussein and his Iraqi troops invaded Kuwait. The United States and its allies issued an ultimatum for his withdrawal, setting a deadline of January 15, 1991, for Iraq to pull out. Iraq didn't. So our armed forces gathered themselves together and turned loose an operation called "Desert Storm."

Then four years later came Wednesday morning, April 19, 1995. At 9:02 a.m. an explosion ripped through the Alfred P. Murrah Federal Building in Oklahoma City, killing 168 men, women, and children.

But we didn't have time to reflect on that one too much, because we were too busy watching a white Bronco make its way down the streets of Los Angeles. And we kept right on following it until Tuesday, October 3, 1995, at around 1 p.m. It seemed like everyone in America stopped what they were doing and gathered around a TV or a radio to hear the verdict on O. J. Simpson.

Then in 1997 stories related to the Space Station Mir and Hurricane Erica were pushed aside by the death of two women who had, in their own distinctive ways, touched the world. One was a young princess named Diana; the other was an old saint named Teresa.

If that wasn't enough for us to take in a ten-year window, in 1998 we were introduced to a twenty-four-year-old White House intern by the name of Monica Lewinsky. And before you knew it, we had a scandal involving the president of the United States that led to a special prosecutor and impeachment hearings.

Tucked away between those headlines was:

the emergence of rap music

the videotaped beating of Rodney King

Clarence Thomas and Anita Hill

"safe sex"

mass murderer Jeffrey Dahmer

the Dream Team in basketball

the bombing of the World Trade Center

David Koresh and Waco

the Los Angeles earthquake

the Whitewater controversy

the suicide of Kurt Cobain

Newt Gingrich and the Contract with America

the Unabomber

Susan Smith

Ruby Ridge

the Million Man March

Bill Gates and Microsoft

the professional debut of golf phenomenon Tiger Woods

the murder of JonBenét Ramsey

the mass suicide of the Heaven's Gate group

the home run chase between Sammy Sosa and Mark McGwire

the retirement of Michael Jordan

the conflict in Bosnia

the shootings at Columbine High School

the Y2K bug

And that is just from the news.

Our tastes ranged from Pokemon to Melatonin, minivans to the Harry Potter books, the internet to Starbucks. Musically we journeyed from Seattle grunge groups like Nirvana and Pearl Jam to, and I know it's hard for us to admit it, the Macarena. Hollywood introduced us to Hannibal Lecter, Jurassic Park, and a young Darth Vader. And we spent time thinking about nothing at all on the show that said it was about nothing at all: *Seinfeld*.

And as we've learned, something else significant happened during that decade: the *nones*—those self-identifying as having no religious affiliation—began a staggeringly fast growth track in the United States. Harvard professor Robert Putnam agrees, tying it to a rebellion of sorts, particularly among the Millennials. He says:

> It begins to jump at around 1990. . . . These were the kids who were coming of age in the America of the culture wars, in the America in which religion publicly became associated with a particular brand of politics, and so I think the single most important reason for the rise of the unknowns is that combination of the younger people moving to the left on social issues and the most visible religious leaders moving to the right on that same issue.[4]

A new perfect storm was forming.

The New Storm

The latest storm is different in form but just as deadly in effect. Rather than issues related to cosmology, biology, and psychology, the new storm consists of perceptions and, in many cases, a tragic but true set of facts. Christianity is again under fire; not because it is intellectually untenable due to new arguments lodged by the heirs to Darwin or

Freud, but because we are perceived to be overly entangled with law and politics, filled with hateful aggression, and consumed with greed. Or put another way, courtesy of the late Warren Zevon, "lawyers, guns, and money."[5]

Money

The money part is easy to understand. Whether through televangelist transgressions or megapastor materialism, money and religion have seldom been a productive pairing. The most famously egregious in recent history was Jim Bakker, founder and host of the now infamous *PTL Club* television ministry. The rumored extravagance of using donor money for air-conditioned dog houses and gold-plated faucets became emblematic of the widespread corruption present in the lives of many televangelists and Christian leaders. More were disgusted by Bakker's materialism and the financial fraud that eventually sent him to prison than by his sexual mishaps, with PTL being lampooned as meaning "Pass the Loot" instead of "Praise the Lord." The irony of the contest of his fated liaison wasn't lost on biographers, such as Charles Shepard. He notes that on the day of Bakker's sexual tryst with a secretary in Clearwater, Florida, he was in the midst of raising even more money through a telethon.[6]

But less known and now even more telling, is how lawyers and guns have come alongside money to form a perfect storm, leading people away from religion altogether into the realm of the *nones*. As the research of the Pew Forum on Religion and Public Life found, "They think that religious organizations are too concerned with money and power, too focused on rules and too involved in politics."[7]

Lawyers

According to a team of sociologists from the University of California, Berkeley, and Duke University, the rise of the *nones* is directly tied to politics. "This is a product of the involvement of the religious right in American politics," notes Claude Fischer, one of the researchers with UC Berkeley, "and the increasing connection in Americans' minds, the minds of moderates and liberals, that religious equals conservative politics equals religion." Going further, Fischer says,

"Increasingly, people identify and link organized religion with antigay attitudes, sexual conservatism, a whole range of those kinds of social cultural values. One way you can think about it is, this is blowback."[8]

In his book *To Change the World*, sociologist James Davison Hunter critiques the dominant ways Christians have thought about culture and cultural change. He saves his most scathing critique for the use of power through politics, which he finds in almost every approach to cultural engagement currently being offered in American Christianity. All, he maintains, are "marked by a *ressentiment*"—a French word that includes our American idea of *resentment* but also involves anger, envy, hate, rage, and revenge as the motive for political action. "*Ressentiment*," writes Hunter, "is grounded in a narrative of injury or, at least, perceived injury; a strong belief that one has been or is being wronged."[9] Christians, Hunter suggests, have given themselves over to this. We've politicized our faith and stake out our positions in ideological terms. This is as true of the Christian Right as the Christian Left, marking Jim Dobson as much as Jim Wallis. All have reduced the public witness of the church to a political witness.

I have previously written of the failed and faulty effort of Christians to "recapture" the culture.[10] Much of this was rooted in the idea that ours was once a Christian nation, and we should actively work to return our governing bodies and laws to their original intent. And even among those who would not espouse a sense of *returning*, there is often a deep sense of fulfilling a Christian destiny. The idea of being "chosen" and receiving a "special blessing" from God has been a constant theme throughout the history of the United States, beginning with the Puritans and their desire that, in the words of John Winthrop in 1630, "wee shall be as a Citty upon a Hill."[11] As historian Conrad Cherry writes, "Throughout their history Americans have been possessed by an acute sense of divine election. They have fancied themselves a New Israel, a people chosen for the awesome responsibility of serving as a light to the nations. . . . It has long been . . . the essence of America's motivating mythology."[12]

The vision of a Christian America was again popularized in the late 1970s by evangelical authors Peter Marshall and David Manuel in *The Light and the Glory*. Marshall and Manuel held that America was founded as a Christian nation and flourished under the benevolent hand of divine providence, arguing further that America's blessings will remain only as long as America as a nation is faithful to God. In 1989 a team of evangelical historians (Mark Noll, Nathan Hatch, and George Marsden) attempted to lay this somewhat dubious thesis to rest, but it continues as a popular framework for viewing American history among American evangelicals.[13]

The Moral Majority of the 1980s found its genesis in such sentiments, and it accordingly formed a top-down strategy for cultural change. If we could only have Christians in the White House, Congress, and the Supreme Court, or populating other leadership elites, then morality would be enacted and faith would once again find the fertile soil needed to establish its footing in individual lives. The Moral Majority won through the election of Ronald Reagan as president, and his subsequent Supreme Court appointments throughout the 1980s brought great anticipation for substantive change.

Yet there has been little real change to mark as a result. Even the prime target—the striking down of the Supreme Court decision *Roe v. Wade*, which legalized abortion—remains the law of the land to this day. Further, the culture wars of the 1980s and '90s are now widely viewed as one of the more distasteful episodes in recent memory, and many younger evangelicals want nothing to do with what was often its caustic, abrasive, and unloving approach toward those apart from Christ. So the effort to recapture the nation failed as a strategy and alienated a younger generation.

Guns

And what of the *guns* dynamic? Many of those outside the Christian faith think Christians no longer represent what Jesus had in mind and that Christianity in our society is not what it was meant to be. We're seen as hyperpolitical, out of touch, pushy in our beliefs, and arrogant. And the most dominant perceptions of all are that we are homophobic, hypocritical, and judgmental. Simply put, in the minds of many, modern-day Christianity no longer seems Christian.

In a video that's been viewed half a million times on YouTube, songwriter and comedian Tim Minchin asks a Sydney, Australia, audience, "Are you up for a sing?"

Minchin begins to sing, "I love Jesus, I love Jesus." Prompting the audience to join him, "Who do you love? Sing it!" Soon the whole crowd is involved, singing "I love Jesus, I love Jesus." Then Minchin changes the lyrics: "I love Jesus, I hate faggots."

The crowd stops singing along.

Minchin looks up from his guitar as if he doesn't understand the nature of the problem. "What happened? I just lost you there," he says. After a halfhearted attempt to get the group singing again, he gives up. "Ah, well." He shrugs. "Maybe these are ideas best shared in churches."[14]

Much of that image has been earned. We've acted in ways, talked in ways, and lived in ways that have stolen from God's reputation. All this and more has flowed from the research of Gabe Lyons and David Kinnaman on how people view the church and people in it.[15] The heart of what they've found is that among young American "outsiders" (that is, those outside the church), the following words or phrases were offered as possible descriptors of Christianity along with the percent who affirmed their accuracy.

antihomosexual (91 percent)

judgmental (87 percent)

hypocritical (85 percent)

old-fashioned (78 percent)

too involved in politics (75 percent)

out of touch with reality (72 percent)

insensitive to others (70 percent)

boring (68 percent)

not accepting of other faiths (64 percent)

confusing (61 percent)

Twenty years ago I commissioned a similar study of people who were unchurched. I asked them a simple question: How did the church and those inside it lose you? I first published the research, done in coordination with the Barna Research Group, in my book *Rethinking the Church*. Comparing the two studies is interesting.

In 1992, the unchurched gave the following reasons for abandoning the church:

there is no value in attending church (74 percent)
churches have too many problems (61 percent)
I do not have the time (48 percent)
I am simply not interested (42 percent)
churches ask for money too frequently (40 percent)
church services are usually boring (36 percent)
Christian churches hold no relevance for the way I live (34 percent)
I do not believe in God; or, I am unsure that God exists (12 percent)

Such findings pointed to a culture that was saying, "God, yes; church, no." That was twenty years ago. Now research shows the deepening crisis because it points to a culture that says, "God, perhaps; Christianity and Christians, no." The idea of even considering church is seemingly off the table.

Modern Assaults on Faith: The second "perfect storm"

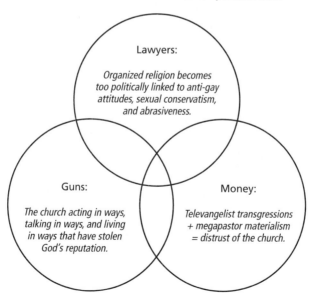

Questions for Discussion and Reflection

1. Both the ARIS report and the Pew report, which documented the rise of the *nones*, found that the secular boom actually happened during the 1990s. Did you sense this happening during that time period? What clued you in to it?

2. One study conducted by a team from the University of California, Berkeley, and Duke University found that the rise of the *nones* is directly related to politics. Individuals link religious affiliation with such sentiments as antigay attitudes and sexual conservatism. How did the role of Christianity in politics through the 1980s and '90s lead to the reduction of the public witness of the church to nothing more than a political witness?

3. The culture wars of the 1980s and '90s left an entire generation of young Americans wanting nothing to do with organized religion, especially if politics was involved. How can you reach out to those who were alienated by the bickering and abrasive language of the culture wars?

4. The biggest perception of Christians today is that they are homophobic, hypocritical, and judgmental. Basically, Christians without the Christ. Are you actively seeking to counter that perception in your life? Is it possible to do more to lower the protective walls of those in your community?

5. The final sentence in the chapter states, "The idea of even considering church is seemingly off the table." What does that say to your heart, mind, and soul about how you approach evangelism today?

6. Do you encounter the "lawyers, guns, and money" mentality in your everyday life? How do you feel when that happens?

7. In the last twelve months, how many sermons or messages have been given in your church that addressed at least one of the perceptions of money, politics, or hate?

4

A Post-Christian World

When America's second president, John Adams, and America's third president, Thomas Jefferson, both died on the same day in 1826—and that day being none other than the Fourth of July—it was seen as a sign of God's favor on the United States. As historian David McCullough notes in his widely acclaimed biography of Adams, it "could not be seen as a mere coincidence: it was a 'visible and palpable' manifestation of 'Divine favor,' wrote John Quincy in his diary that night, expressing," McCullough adds, "what was felt and would be said again and again everywhere the news spread."[1]

As mentioned in the previous chapter, the idea of being "chosen" and receiving a "special blessing" from God has been a constant theme throughout the history of the United States, beginning with the Puritans and their "city on a shining hill."[2] Yet however you view America's spiritual history, one thing is certain: today, America is not a Christian nation. This does not mean it is non-Christian or anti-Christian, simply that it has joined the ranks of many other Western countries and is *post*-Christian. To be post-Christian means that the very memory of the gospel is becoming nonexistent.[3]

Recent research by the Barna Group has tried to define and quantify Americans' various stages of nonbelief. In other words, Who is post-Christian? Digging deeper than what people may label themselves (e.g., *nones*), they wanted to also account for belief and behavior. This is critical since more than seven out of ten Americans describe themselves as "Christian," and more than six out of every ten say they are "deeply spiritual."

As a result, the Barna Group employed the following fifteen measurements:

1. Do not believe in God
2. Identify as atheist or agnostic
3. Disagree that faith is important in their lives
4. Have not prayed to God (in the last year)
5. Have never made a commitment to Jesus
6. Disagree the Bible is accurate
7. Have not donated money to a church (in the last year)
8. Have not attended a Christian church (in the last year)
9. Agree that Jesus committed sins
10. Do not feel a responsibility to "share their faith"
11. Have not read the Bible (in the last week)
12. Have not volunteered at church (in the last week)
13. Have not attended Sunday school (in the last week)
14. Have not attended a religious small group (in the last week)
15. Have not participated in a house church (in the last year)

To be deemed "post-Christian," the person had to meet 60 percent or more of the fifteen factors. To be deemed "highly post-Christian," the person had to meet at least 80 percent (twelve or more) of the factors. Examining these fifteen measures of nonreligiosity, they found that 37 percent of Americans are generally post-Christian, and one in four (25 percent) are highly post-Christian.[4]

Cause or Effect?

Does this play into the rise of the *nones*? Is the ever-deepening post-Christian reality of America causing the rise, or is the rise itself the cause of the growing post-Christian milieu? Or neither?

The Pew Forum study suggested that one of the forces behind the rise of the religiously unaffiliated is generational replacement. This simply refers to the gradual supplanting of older generations by newer ones. While true, it is not a causal connection. It simply explains why the numbers are on the rise. For example, only one in twenty members of the World War II–era Greatest Generation—or 5 percent—could be classified among the *nones*. Compare that to younger Millennials (those ages eighteen through twenty-three), who were minors during earlier studies and thus not able to be interviewed. Of this younger demographic which is now being folded into national averages, a full one-third (34 percent) are religiously unaffiliated.[5]

So what is causing later generations to enter the ranks of the *nones* in such large numbers? Yes, generational replacement is affecting the numbers, but why the generational disconnect with religion?

Percentage of "Nones" by Generation

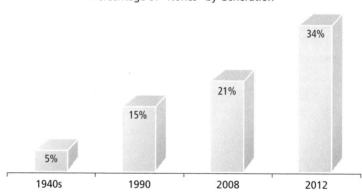

| 1940s | 1990 | 2008 | 2012 |

A further reason to look to wider cultural dynamics is that Gen Xers and baby boomers also have become more religiously unaffiliated in recent years. In 2012, the Pew Forum found that 21 percent of Gen Xers and 15 percent of baby boomers (a 3 percent increase among each generation from 2007) placed themselves among the *nones*. Further, the overwhelming majority of all of the *nones* were brought up in a religious tradition.[6]

No, what is at hand is something more. Sociologist Peter Berger, among many others, has long suggested that the modern world is being shaped by three deep and fast-moving cultural currents: secularization, privatization, and pluralization.[7] Big words. Even bigger ideas. But it's within these words and ideas that we find the wider cultural key to the rise of the *nones*.[8]

The Process of Secularization

The English word *secular* is derived from the Latin *saeculum*, which means "this present age." The contemporary term *secular* is descriptive, referring to that which is divorced from religious or spiritual sensibility. Looking back to the ancient Latin usage, it instead enthrones that which is of this world. Secularization is the *process* by which something *becomes* secular. It is the cultural current making things secular.

And it is raging through our world like a flash flood.

Berger defines secularization as the process by which "sectors of society and culture are removed from the domination of religious institutions and symbols."[9] The effect of this process is that the church is losing its influence as a shaper of life and thought in the wider social order, and Christianity is losing its place as the dominant worldview. Richard John Neuhaus writes that we live in a "naked public square," meaning that religious ideas and mores no longer inform public discourse.[10] Christianity has ceased to be the motivating center of Western life; the religious question is consciously or unconsciously pushed from the heart of human concerns, and the institutional forms of Christianity have, and are, undergoing revision at the hands of the world.[11]

In his *Guide for the Perplexed*, author E. F. Schumacher relates his experience of getting lost during a sightseeing trip to Moscow during the Stalinist era. Trying to get his bearings, he found himself standing with several large churches within his line of sight. Yet none of these churches were found on his map. An interpreter came to assist him and explained, "We don't show churches on our maps."

Schumacher contradicted the interpreter by quickly pointing out a church that was clearly marked on his map.

"That is a museum," the interpreter said, "not what we call a 'living church.' It is only the 'living churches' we don't show."

That, Schumacher goes on to conclude, was the cultural point. Those things that mankind has most believed in are no longer on the map of reality, or if they are, they are relegated to a museum.[12] In reflecting on Schumacher's story, Huston Smith notes that our world "has erased transcendence from our reality map."[13] Or as C. S. Lewis observes, "Almost all our modern philosophies have been devised to convince us that the good of man is to be found on this earth."[14]

Yet a full-blown secularization *thesis* has been challenged.[15] Not the reality of the process itself; Christian Smith notes that no matter where one stands on its impact, "Something real at the level of macrosocial change . . . has actually happened in history."[16] What is debated is the degree to which the process of secularization can redirect a person away from a belief in God. This argument is clearly in question in the United States, for while the process of secularization is clear, it has yet to produce an overwhelmingly secularized population. German philosopher Friedrich Nietzsche may have proclaimed God dead, but it could be contended that few in America attended the wake. Our day is, as Peter Berger himself observes, "as furiously religious as it ever was, and in some places more so than ever."[17]

But that is where Berger is wrong. We may not be losing our belief in God, but we are losing our religion. While we may not be turning into atheists, we seem quite content to accept the idea of faith being privately engaging but culturally irrelevant. And yes, this is because of the process of secularization.

Consider the secularized subculture currently resting at the top of the American educational system, the media of mass communication, and the upper echelons of the legal system. These are the epicenters of culture and the means by which values and ideas come into being and are disseminated. While their forces may be "relatively thin on the ground," Berger observes, "they are very influential, as they control the institutions that provide the 'official' definitions of reality."[18]

Think about how faith itself is tended. It needs *support*. Apart from a Christian community, we quickly wither. We need a context of encouragement. Beliefs don't exist in a vacuum; they need to be nurtured, reinforced. A secularized world no longer offers the deep religious socialization and the frequent reaffirmation of beliefs necessary for a distinctive faith to flourish. The declining social significance of religion will inevitably cause a decline in the *number* of religious people and the *extent* to which those people are religious. When society no longer supports religious affirmation, the difficulty of maintaining individual faith increases dramatically. "To be sustained and kept intact, [a religion] must be cultivated and guarded. When it is very widely shared and thoroughly embedded in everyday life and in powerful social institutions, there is little danger it will disappear," sociologist Steve Bruce observes. "The problem arises when the surrounding society is becoming secular."[19]

As a result, we should not be surprised at the rise of the *nones*—or when their ranks continue to swell.

The Process of Privatization

Ray Kroc, the man who turned McDonald's into a fast-food franchise, has said, "I believe in God, family, and McDonald's. And in the office, that order is reversed."[20]

Not many in our world would find fault with his approach. Privatization is the process by which a chasm is created between the public and the private spheres of life, and spiritual things are increasingly placed within the private arena.[21] So when it comes to things like business, politics, or even marriage and the home, personal faith is bracketed off. The process of privatization, left unchecked, makes the Christian faith a matter of personal preference, trivialized to the realm of taste or opinion.[22] This trend was evident to historian Theodore Roszak who, after traveling to America, remarked that Christian faith in America was one that was "socially irrelevant, even if privately engaging."[23]

The influence of privatization is profound. Faith does not simply have a new home in our private lives; it is no longer accepted outside of that sphere. More than showing poor form, talk of faith has been banished from the wider public agenda. As historian and educator Page Smith sarcastically observed, in our day "God is not a proper topic for conversation, but 'lesbian politics' is."[24] But privatization goes further. Once placed solely within our private world, faith becomes little more than a reflection of ourselves. Spirituality has become anything an individual desires it to be—a private affair to be developed as one sees fit.

It is precisely this context that has compelled so many to move into the *nones*. Religion is, if anything, a public sphere manifestation of faith, and yet we don't want faith in the public sphere. Further, if we subscribe to a defined set of beliefs or historic links to orthodoxy, our private world faith is held accountable—which is exactly what is least desired. So privatization is at war with what the establishment of religion requires, which is why the rise of the *nones* has benefitted so much from this current's coursing.

The Process of Pluralization

I'm a fan of the old *Andy Griffith* TV series. Near my home in Charlotte is Mt. Airy, North Carolina—the real hometown of Andy Griffith and the inspiration for Mayberry. The small hamlet annually holds a Mayberry Days festival that attracts thousands. One year my family and I went, and we could readily see how the little town had shaped the series. The quaint downtown, the diner—there was even a Floyd's Barber Shop.

If you've ever watched the series, still in heavy syndication, you know that when Andy's deputy, Barney Fife, asked his longtime girlfriend, Thelma Lou, out for a date, more often than not it was, "Want to go to the picture?" This meant the movie at the movie theater. Which movie would they see? *The* movie. There was only one. It changed

---

Three Moving Cultural Currents

1. Secularization: The church is losing its influence as a shaper of life and thought in the wider social order, and Christianity is losing its place as the dominant worldview.
2. Privatization: A chasm is created between the public and the private spheres of life, and spiritual things are increasingly placed within the private arena.
3. Pluralization: Individuals are confronted with a staggering number of ideologies and faith options competing for their attention.

from time to time, causing an excited stir among the residents and an occasion for another outing, but there would only be *one* film showing.

Barney and Thelma Lou would have a time of it now. We go to a Cineplex and choose from twenty or more films—each one assaulting our senses through marketing and promotion. Then there's Netflix, which offers thousands more, streaming via the internet. The simple "Want to go to the picture?" isn't so simple anymore. It's not even the right question. This is the heart of pluralization. The process of pluralization occurs when individuals are confronted with a staggering number of ideologies and faith options competing for their attention.[25] Pluralization is that process by which the number of options for our private sphere to consider multiplies explosively—particularly at the level of worldviews and faith.[26] Peter Berger speaks of the traditional role of religion as a "sacred canopy" covering the contemporary culture. Religion, at least in terms of the idea of there being a God whom life and thought had to consider, blanketed all of society and culture. Today that canopy is gone, replaced instead by millions of small tents under which we can choose to dwell.[27]

There can be little doubt that the fuel that powered this process, at least in the United States, was immigration. One visit to Ellis Island will drive this home, as inside the main visitors center is a visual display of the tidal wave of immigration that struck upon the shores of our country. Between 1901 and 1910, nearly nine million immigrants were admitted to the United States, the majority from Southern and Eastern Europe. Nearly six million more came during the following decade. By 1910, 40 percent of the population of New York City was foreign-born.[28] And they brought their religions with them.

But the process of pluralization means far more than a simple increase in the number of faith options. The sheer number of choices and competing ideologies suggests that no one perspective or religious persuasion has the inside track about the spiritual realm.[29] Theologian Langdon Gilkey is correct when he observes that "many religions have always existed"; what is different is a "new consciousness" that "entails a feeling of rough parity, as well as diversity, among religion." By *parity*, Gilkey means "the presence of both truth and grace in other ways."[30] Harold O. J. Brown adds that such pluralism is actually "value pluralism," meaning that "all convictions about values are of

Ellis Island

equal validity, which says in effect that no convictions about values have any validity."[31]

This has fostered a smorgasbord mentality in regard to the construction of personal beliefs. Malise Ruthven calls America the "divine supermarket." The technical term is *syncretism*, the mix-and-match mentality of pulling together different threads in various religions in order to create a personal religion that suits our individual taste. Christianity becomes one of many competing boutique worldviews, no better or worse than another, that have set up shop in society's mall for people to sample as a matter of personal preference.

So while Christianity used to be rejected by Enlightenment intellectuals because they thought its central beliefs had been disproven by science or philosophy, today orthodox Christianity tends to be disqualified on the grounds that it argues for a truth that is unchanging and universal.[32] A particular faith used to be wrong on the basis of what one perceived to be truth; now a faith is wrong for claiming there *is* truth. As Allan Bloom wryly notes, "The true believer is the real danger."[33] Again, this is fueling the rise of those who hesitate to say they believe in any specific religion.

Without God, Without Creed

Is this all that has happened? No. While culture has become more secularized, privatized, and pluralized, so has religion itself.

In what I consider an overlooked book, *Without God, Without Creed: The Origins of Unbelief in America*, James Turner argues that unbelief is not something that has happened *to* religion. Instead, he argues, religion has helped cause unbelief. "In trying to adapt their religious beliefs to socioeconomic change, to new moral challenges, to novel problems of knowledge, to the tightening standards of science, the defenders of God slowly strangled Him." Specifically, many who believed decided "to deal with modernity by embracing it—to defuse modern threats to the traditional bases of belief by bringing God into line with modernity." In so doing, they forgot that

> God's purposes were not supposed to be man's. . . . They forgot, in short, that their God was . . . radically other than man. . . . Unbelief emerged because church leaders too often forgot the transcendence essential to any worthwhile God. They committed religion *functionally* to making the world better in human terms and *intellectually* to modes of knowing God fitted only for understanding this world.[34]

Mark Silk, director of the Greenberg Center for the Study of Religion in Public Life at Trinity College, seems to be in agreement with Turner's thesis, noting that there is a "considerable softening of the edges in doctrine, politics and social values" contributing to the rise of the *nones*.[35] So little wonder that a study by the Rasmussen Reports polling, released on Good Friday of 2013, found that only 64 percent of Americans believe that Jesus Christ rose from the dead, down from 77 percent only a year before.[36]

This has created the *spiritual without being religious* mentality that sounds very good on the surface but translates into a pseudo-spirituality that is without content and is filled with little more than our personal meaning. Paul M. Zulehner, dean of Vienna University's divinity school and one of the world's most distinguished sociologists of religion, maintains that a "false spirituality" is rising that will prove to be "a more dangerous rival to the Christian faith than atheism."[37]

Questions for Discussion and Reflection

1. America is no longer a Christian nation. Have you ever paused to consider this new reality?

2. The reality is that America is now a post-Christian nation, meaning the very memory of the gospel is becoming nonexistent. Have you changed your reality to match the new landscape of American Christianity?

3. Within the Millennials, those ages eighteen through twenty-three, one-third are religiously unaffiliated. This means young people today have far less knowledge of the gospel than previous generations. How can this lack of knowledge be addressed by the ministry offerings at your church?

4. What is the process of secularization?

5. In the preceding pages, we learned that the current of secularization is raging through our world. Where do you see this happening around you?

6. American Christians seem content with accepting the idea of a private faith that is culturally irrelevant. Do you live your own life with this same sentiment? How can you encourage your community to move out of this idea and into the Great Commission?

7. The process of moving faith into the private sector and out of the public is called *privatization*. The idea is one of comfort since it does not require much of us in public. But once this happens and faith lives only in a person's private world, it becomes nothing more than a reflection of that individual. What are the problems with this kind of faith?

8. Our culture is a pluralized one, meaning there are a number of options to consider when it comes to your private life. How do you see this play out in the world around you?

9. The sheer number of ideologies in the marketplace of ideas suggests, especially to *nones*, that no one has a monopoly on the spiritual realm. What can be done to address this notion at your church?

5

Bad Religion

In Ross Douthat's book *Bad Religion*, the *New York Times* columnist offers a synopsis of the core beliefs of America's wave of "spiritual but not religious" teachers such as Deepak Chopra, James Redfield, Eckhart Tolle, Paulo Coelho, Neale Donald Walsch, Oprah Winfrey, and Elizabeth Gilbert. According to Douthat, their "creed" shares four beliefs.[1]

1. *All organized religions offer only partial glimpses of God (or Light or Being).* Thus, we must seek to experience God through feeling rather than reason, through experience rather than dogma, through a direct encounter rather than a hand-me-down revelation. As Neale Donald Walsch writes in his book *Conversations with God*, "Listen to your feelings. Listen to your Highest Thought. . . . Whenever any of these differ from what you've been told by your teachers, or read in your books, forget the words."[2]

2. *God is everywhere and within everything—especially within you.* You can encounter God by getting in touch with the divinity who resides inside your very self and soul. At the climax of his book, *The Alchemist*, Paulo Coelho writes: "The boy reached through the Soul of the World, and saw that it was a part of the Soul of God. And he saw that the Soul of God was his own soul."[3]

3. *Sin and evil are largely illusions that will ultimately be reconciled rather than defeated.* There is no hell save the one we make for ourselves

on earth—no final separation from the Being within whom all our beings rest. Elizabeth Gilbert assures her readers, "There is no such thing
in this universe as hell, except maybe in our own terrified minds."[4]

4. *Perfect happiness is available right now.* Heaven is on earth. Eter-
nity can be entered at any moment, by any person who understands
how to let go, let God, and let himself or herself be washed away
in love. James Redfield writes, "At some point everyone will vibrate
highly enough so that we can walk into heaven, in our same form."
And Coelho adds, "I do believe in life after death, but I also don't
think that it's that important. What's important is to understand that
we are also living this life after death now."[5]

I have written similarly of the "Church of Oprah-Wan Kenobi"
and the rise of a new New Age movement that is based largely on
popularized Hinduism, which is what Douthat has described. But
what Douthat, myself, and others have actually detailed is the official
religion of the cultural epicenters, namely media. It is not the official
religion of the religiously unaffiliated. At least not yet.

The Pew Forum study, among others, has found that the ranks
of the unaffiliated are not predominantly composed of New Age
spirituality or alternative forms of religion. Generally speaking, the
unaffiliated are no more likely than members of the public as a whole
to have such beliefs and practices. That means that approximately
three in ten say they believe in spiritual energy in physical objects and
in yoga as a spiritual practice. Around a quarter believe in astrology
and reincarnation. Six in ten say they have a deep connection with
nature and the earth. About three in ten say they have felt in touch
with someone who is dead, and 15 percent have consulted a psychic.
All of these figures closely resemble the public as a whole.[6]

The importance of knowing the "bad religion" advertised through
popular culture is the effect it will inevitably have on the religiously
unaffiliated as they separate from religion itself. Right now they do
not seem to be any more affected than people of defined faith, but
that is arguably the strength of their, largely, Christian memory. Most
of the newly unaffiliated were part of a Christian faith tradition that
was anything but Eastern in orientation. Once untethered from these
moorings, whether Catholicism or Protestantism, they will be more
susceptible to the prevailing views of culture. Our inner worlds abhor
a vacuum; we will fill it with something.

> ## Views of the Religiously Unaffiliated
>
> - Three out of ten believe in a spiritual energy in physical objects and in yoga as a spiritual practice.
> - 25 percent believe in astrology and reincarnation.
> - Six out of ten say they have a deep connection with nature and the earth.
> - Three out of ten have felt "in touch" with someone who is dead.
> - 15 percent have consulted a psychic.

But while pop-Hinduism may not have made inroads into the unaffiliated as yet, there is another bad religion that *is* firmly entrenched: a truthy, wiki dogma for mistakers.

Truthiness

The first headline related to the belief system of the *nones* is that the unaffiliated tend to believe there is a lot of truth to go around. There isn't just one truth out there; there are multiple truths.

I once read a children's book, supporting a PBS series, written by a Jewish rabbi and a Catholic monsignor. In it they wrote that searching for God has become like climbing a mountain. Since everyone *knows* that there is not just *one* way to climb a mountain—mountains are simply too big for that—there are any number of paths that can be taken. So, the rabbi and priest concluded, all of the ideas about God throughout the religions of the world are like different ways up the mountain, and all of the names of God in all of the world's religions all name the same God. The Dalai Lama, who wrote the foreword to the book, agreed.[7]

But it's not simply the idea of multiple truths; it's also about what that idea produces. If you believe that truth is everywhere, making truth mean very little, what does that leave you with? A word first introduced by comedian Stephen Colbert: *truthiness*.[8] Here's how Colbert described it:

> And that brings us to tonight's word: truthiness.
>
> Now, I'm sure some of the Word Police, the "wordanistas" over at Webster's, are gonna say, "Hey, that's not a word." Well, anybody who

knows me knows that I'm no fan of dictionaries or reference books. They are elitist. Constantly telling us what is or isn't true, or what did or didn't happen. Who's Britannica to tell me the Panama Canal was finished in 1914? If I wanna say it happened in 1941, that's my right. I don't trust books. They're all fact, not heart.[9]

The idea behind *truthiness* is that actual facts don't matter. What matters is how you feel, for you as an individual are the final arbiter of truth. *Truthiness* is the bald assertion that we are not only to discern truth for ourselves *from* the facts at hand, but also to create truth for ourselves *despite* the facts at hand.[10] We so felt the truth of Colbert's satire that *truthiness* later became *Oxford American Dictionary*'s word of the year. That brings us to another word, and once again, courtesy of Mr. Colbert: *wikiality*.[11]

Wikiality

Among the internet's most popular sites is Wikipedia, the online encyclopedia that is written entirely by unpaid volunteers. Though praised for "democratizing knowledge" by such luminaries as Stanford University law professor Lawrence Lessig, Wikipedia has more than its fair share of detractors. In 2006 the site drew unwanted attention when journalist John Seigenthaler exposed gross errors and fabrications in the biographical entry on his life. Numerous scholars have voiced concern that the encyclopedia is an unreliable research tool and lament students' use of the resource. A paper by a University of California at Merced graduate student revealed many of Wikipedia's flaws, including often indifferent prose and some serious problems with accuracy.[12]

Yet it seems Wikipedia is here to stay. In 2013 the ninth annual Wikimania conference—a five-day discussion of the Wikimedia Foundation's various projects—was held in Hong Kong. In addition, the English-language version of Wikipedia has surpassed four million articles; there are over twenty-six million articles across all languages; and it is consistently one of the Web's twenty most popular destinations.[13]

Regardless of the accuracy of certain articles, and separate from the movement advocating free access to information online, Stephen Colbert has put his finger on the real issue in his play off of the word *reality*. *Wikiality* is defined as "reality as determined by majority vote," such as when astronomers voted Pluto off their list of planets. Colbert notes that with Wikipedia, any user can log on and make a change on any entry, and if enough users agree, it becomes true. Colbert muses about a *wikiality* where this could apply to the entire body of human knowledge. "Together we can create a reality we can all agree on. The reality we just agreed on."[14] So through a new "wikiality," we can take our collective "truthiness" and make it "fact" for all through majority vote.

With such democratization of knowledge comes the democratization of truth, resulting in an evolution from the idea that "what is true for you is true for you, and what is true for me is true for me" to the new belief that "what is true for us is true for us." And there would be no reason not to hold to its corollary: "and what is true for them is true for them." In a "wiki" world, there is no truth outside of what the majority determines. Fifty-one percent become the final arbiter of reality. The idea of truth finally becomes divorced from any kind of mooring—it simply drifts along the breezes of cultural mores. Or as Marshall Poe observes in the *Atlantic*, "If the community changes its mind and decides that two plus two equals five, then *two plus two does equal five*."[15]

This is reflected comically in the movie *Talladega Nights* during a prayer before family dinner led by race-car driver Ricky Bobby (played by Will Ferrell), who decides he wants to pray to Jesus as a baby.[16] This opens the door to an interesting theological discussion between Ricky Bobby; his two sons; his wife, Carley; her father; and Ricky Bobby's best friend, Cal:

Ricky Bobby: Dear Tiny Infant Jesus—

Carley: Hey, umm, you know, sweetie, Jesus did grow up. You don't always have to call him "baby." It's a bit odd and off-putting praying to a baby.

Ricky Bobby: I like the Christmas Jesus best and I'm saying grace. When you're saying grace, you can say it to grown-up Jesus, or teenage Jesus, or bearded Jesus, or whoever you want.

(returning to his prayer) . . . Dear Tiny Jesus, with your golden-fleeced diapers, with your tiny little fat, balled-up fists—

Carley's father: He was a man; he had a beard!

Ricky Bobby: Look, I like the baby version the best. Do you hear me? I win the races and I get the money . . .

Cal: I like to picture Jesus in a tuxedo T-shirt, 'cause it says, like, I want to be formal, but I'm here to party too. 'Cause I like to party, so I like my Jesus to party.

Walker (son): I like to picture Jesus as a ninja fightin' off evil Samurai.

Cal: I like to think of Jesus with, like, with giant eagles' wings singin' lead vocals for Lynyrd Skynyrd with, like, an angel band. And I'm in the front row and I'm hammered drunk . . .

Ricky Bobby (continuing to pray): Dear eight-pound six-ounce, new-born infant Jesus, don't even know a word yet . . . thank you for all your power and your grace, dear baby God. Amen.[17]

Such pick-and-choose approaches to truth are not without their cultural critics. Consider the recent release of Malcolm Gladwell's book *David and Goliath*. In his bestselling titles such as *The Tipping Point*, *Blink*, and *Outliers*, Gladwell's approach has been to popularize various research projects and draw counterintuitive conclusions. Now, I am a fan of Gladwell and find that his writings offer interesting challenges to conventional wisdom. Yet reviews of his work point out that the research he reveals is often small, unverified, or contradicted by larger and more established studies. Further, the conclusions he draws as the "only" conclusion are far from it.[18]

For example, he writes how a disproportionate number of eminent people lost a parent in childhood, and he draws the conclusion that such adversity strengthens someone for success. Yet in another section, Gladwell notes that prisoners are also far more likely than the general population to have suffered that blow as children. So which is it? Do early wounds create winners, except when they don't? Gladwell's approach is said to involve telling "just-so stories and cherry-picking science to back them" and starting off with "the fallacy of the unexamined premise." More to the point, what "he presents are mostly just intriguing possibilities and musings about human behavior, but what his publisher sells them as, and what his readers may incorrectly take them for, are lawful, causal rules that explain how the world really works."[19]

It's a wiki approach, to be sure, which may be why it's made him one of the biggest selling authors of nonfiction in the Western world. After all, it's a wiki world.

Mistakers

So what does all this mean for the unaffiliated and how they view their moral world? Once you get rid of true and false, you also tend to get rid of right and wrong.

This was first forecast back in 1973 when psychiatrist Karl Menninger published a book entitled *Whatever Became of Sin?* His point was that sociology and psychology were beginning to avoid terms like *evil*, *immorality*, and *wrongdoing*. Menninger then detailed how the theological notion of sin became the legal idea of crime and then slid further from its true meaning and became nothing more than the psychological category of sickness.[20]

Now it's gone even further. We're not sinners at all anymore. As many have observed, we're just *mistakers*. And we're even starting to lose that. Lately, we don't even want to call a sin a mistake. We want to turn everything we do into a virtue. So lust becomes "sensuality," and anger just means "being honest with your emotions." Even when we apologize, we say things like, "I'm sorry you were offended by what I said or did." No admittance that we did anything wrong—just sorry that the other person wasn't mature enough to handle it. The latest edition of the *Oxford Junior Dictionary* for children went all the way and made it official. The compilers removed the word completely. They don't even have the word *sin* in the dictionary anymore.[21]

As a result, morals are seen as almost entirely relative. There are no absolutes when it comes to right or wrong. If it doesn't hurt anybody else and it makes you happy, then it's okay. Morality has become a personal choice. It's personal, private, subjective, and a matter of personal decision or opinion. Consider the following interview with Nick Cassavetes, the director of such films as *The Notebook* and *John Q*. His latest film, *Yellow*, debuted at the Toronto Film Festival.

It's about an incestuous relationship between a brother and a sister. Speaking of incest, Cassavetes offered these thoughts:

> This whole movie is about judgment, and lack of it, and doing what you want. Who gives a [expletive] if people judge you? I'm not saying this is an absolute but in a way, if you're not having kids—who gives a d—? Love who you want. Isn't that what we say? Gay marriage—love who you want? If it's your brother or sister it's super weird, but if you look at it, you're not hurting anybody, except every single person who freaks out because you're in love with one another.[22]

This mindset is documented in sociologist Christian Smith's massive study of emerging adults—people between the ages of eighteen and twenty-three. He found that a relativistic attitude marks six out of ten (60 percent) emerging adults. They said morality is a personal choice, "entirely a matter of individual decision. Moral rights and wrongs are essentially matters of individual opinion." One out of every three said they didn't even know what makes anything right or wrong.[23]

Here it is in their own words:

> "I have never heard anybody else that has anything like it [my moral outlook] and I just don't know where it came from. Like just kinda things that I thought up, that I decided was right for me."[24]

> "What's a moral rule, though? A personal thing? Well then I would say that sometimes breaking a moral rule may be all right, depending on the situation."[25]

> "Wrong are the things that change things for way worse than they were before—and I kinda think again it's totally relative to the person, it depends on where you wanna go and what you wanna do."[26]

> "I don't think lying is wrong necessarily. It's life. People lie. That's my view on the whole thing. Everyone's done it. It's not going to go away."[27]

> "I will do what I can to get ahead in this world while I'm here."[28]

> "I would do what I thought made me happy or how I felt. Because I have no other way of knowing what to do but how I internally feel. That's where my decisions come from. From me. My decisions come from inside of me."[29]

Defining the Belief System of the *Nones*

Truthiness: the assertion that we are not only to discern truth for ourselves *from* the facts at hand, but also to create truth for ourselves *despite* the facts at hand

Wikiality: reality as determined by majority vote, such as when astronomers voted Pluto off their list of planets

Mistakers: to avoid calling ourselves sinners, we've become *mistakers*; to turn everything we do into a virtue where lust becomes "sensuality," and anger is just "being honest with your emotions"

So while the definition of *nones* is that they believe "nothing in particular," in truth, they believe something very particular. It just isn't a belief in truth. Instead, it's more of a belief in themselves. It brings to mind an older study, conducted by sociologist Robert Bellah, that featured an interview with a woman named Sheila, who said, "I believe in God. I'm not a religious fanatic. I can't remember the last time I went to church. My faith has carried me a long way. It's 'Sheilaism.' Just my own little voice."[30]

Questions for Discussion and Reflection

1. The creed of the spiritual but not religious includes the following: all organized religions offer only partial glimpses of God; God is everywhere and in everything; sin and evil are illusions; and perfect happiness is available right now. This creed has a stronghold in cultural epicenters. What can be done to combat these ideas in your church and community?

2. As you read, our inner world abhors a vacuum; we will fill it with something. Does this convict you to spread the gospel? Does it bring a sense of urgency?

3. We live in a world of "truthiness" in which actual facts are becoming increasingly less important, and how you feel as an individual is becoming the determining factor of truth. Why is this important to know? How do you use this understanding to reach the lost?

4. "Wikiality" refers to reality as determined by majority vote. Think of Wikipedia and how its entries are compiled. What is the danger of this phenomenon?

5. The natural progression of "truthiness" and "wikiality" is the belief that "what is true for us is true for us." This is a prevailing sentiment in our culture today. How does this thinking damage the church's witness, and how can it be approached in a loving way by your church?

6. Once truth becomes individualized and it means only what we want it to mean, the concept of right and wrong soon follow. So the very concept of sin—something being wrong according to the will of God—is thrown out the window. Are you helping people realize their sin in a graceful way, or are you affirming their disregard for sin by choosing not to engage the topic?

7. The Bible teaches a moral code that was handed down by God himself, and we should adhere to that code as believers in Christ. With all the shifts in thinking, especially among the *nones*, morality has become a personal choice. What is the role of truth, or the role of God's Word, in breaking through that barrier when speaking to the unchurched?

8. The *nones*, as you just read, actually do believe in something— it's just not truth. They believe in themselves. As church leaders and active members in the church, you have an obligation to show people the truth of Jesus. This will not be easy. In many ways, the gospel runs counter to their thinking, and you have been sent to do just that. Are you prepared to do the work to bring the gospel to these lost sheep? Are you doing the research and prayer necessary?

An Interlude

So there you have it. The rise of the *nones*, why they have risen, and what marks their thinking. But what can be done to reach them? That is what the second part of this book will explore. But first we must ground ourselves in the most significant shift of missional paradigms that has taken place in our day: we have moved from an Acts 2 missional context to an Acts 17 missional context.

Both scenes from the New Testament portray a classic engagement of contemporary culture. In Acts 2, you have Peter before the God-fearing Jews of Jerusalem. His message is easily paraphrased and summarized:

> You know about the creation, Adam and Eve, and the fall; you know about Moses and the Law; you know about Abraham and the chosen people of Israel; you know of the prophets and the promised coming of the Messiah. So we don't need to waste time on that. What you need to know is that Jesus was that Messiah, you rejected him, and now you are in deep weeds and need to repent.

That was it. And three thousand did!

Peter was able to speak to a group of people who were already monotheists, already buying into the Old Testament Scriptures, and already believing in a coming Messiah. Now move to Acts 17:22–31. Paul is on Mars Hill speaking to the philosophers and spiritual theorists of Athens. This was a spiritual marketplace where truth was

Wikimedia Commons

The Temple in Jerusalem

relative, worldviews and gods littered the landscape, and the average person didn't know Abraham from an apricot. He knew he wasn't in Kansas—I mean Jerusalem—anymore. So he didn't take an Acts 2 approach, much less give an Acts 2 message. He had to find a way to connect with the culture, and the people in it. So he looked around and found a touchstone—an altar to an unknown God. The culture was so pluralistic that the only thing they could agree on was that you couldn't know anything for sure.

"What if I could tell you that God's name?" Paul offered. "Would that be of interest?"

Paul then went all the way back to creation and began working his way forward—laying a foundation for an understanding and subsequent engagement of the gospel. He had to. They didn't have any knowledge of the Christian faith to start with.

Like today.

But there is something even beyond the Acts 17 context to consider. With the original Mars Hill, there was rampant ignorance about Christianity, not to mention Judaism. Paul was able to start with a blank slate. In our context today, our culture is post-Christian, not non-Christian. This is a significant difference. In a post-Christian context many believe they *do* know about Christianity—even though it's often a caricature of its true nature—and thus they feel it has been tried and found wanting. Further, the current context continually lampoons the Christian faith while dismissing it as intellectually bereft of weight. There's a *been there, done that* attitude that is often more difficult to overcome than when engaging a pristine mission field. So we have a culture that is post-Christian, yet the people think they know Christianity. Consider it the worst combination of Acts 2 and Acts 17 imaginable.

It is just as important to note what an Acts 17 approach is *not*. It is not simply becoming more hip and trendy, mirroring our culture in ways that make us *fit in*. As Marc Yoder writes in a blog that went viral titled "Top 10 Reasons Our Kids Leave Church,"

> We've taken a historic, 2,000 year old faith, dressed it in plaid and skinny jeans and tried to sell it as "cool" to our kids. It's not cool. It's not modern. What we're packaging is a cheap knockoff. . . .
>   In our effort to be "like them" we've become less of who we actually are. The middle-aged pastor trying to look like his twentysomething audience isn't relevant. Dress him up in skinny jeans and hand him a latte, it doesn't matter. It's not relevant, it's comically cliché.[1]

In another book I have written of this mistaken approach as the attempt to *reflect* culture; like a mirror we reflect culture and its values.[2] Rather than trying to influence culture, we allow culture to influence us. The spirit of this is the attempt to "become all things to all people so that by all possible means" we may save some, as Paul suggests (1 Cor. 9:22). There can be little doubt that evangelical Christianity has been captive in a cultural ghetto of its own making. To break free of such bondage, many have made the effort to build bridges of understanding and relationship. Whether through the use of contemporary music or film, secular venues or vernacular, the goal has been to create a means for connection. So rather than railing against pornography through presidential commissions, there are booths set up at the AVN Adult Entertainment Expo in Las Vegas with the message: "Jesus loves porn stars."[3]

While laudable and often necessary, some efforts at reflection have slid into mere mirroring. Rather than working in and through culture

> Though I am free and belong to no one, I have made myself a slave to everyone, to win as many as possible. To the Jews I became like a Jew, to win the Jews. To those under the law I became like one under the law (though I myself am not under the law), so as to win those under the law. To those not having the law I became like one not having the law (though I am not free from God's law but am under Christ's law), so as to win those not having the law. To the weak I became weak, to win the weak. I have become all things to all people so that by all possible means I might save some.
>
> 1 Corinthians 9:19–22

in the form of, for example, Paul *on* Mars Hill, or creating a Mars Hill culture of dialogue and openness, there is a growing movement that seems to reflect the values of Mars Hill *itself* in order to gain a hearing—actually becoming the people we are attempting to reach and creating cultures that reflect our world rather than building bridges to reach it. Consider the recent blog post of one young Christian leader who, articulating his stance on homosexuality, felt himself

> drifting toward acceptance that gay persons are fully human persons and should be afforded all of the cultural and ecclesial benefits that I am. . . . I now believe that GLBTQ [Gay, Lesbian, Bisexual, Transgender, and Queer] can live lives in accord with biblical Christianity (at least as much as any of us can!) and that their monogamy can and should be sanctioned and blessed by church and state.[4]

Yes to being fully human persons; *no* to GLBTQ who embrace such lifestyles, even in monogamy, living in accord with biblical Christianity and being blessed by the church. Such blessing is not reaching into a culture with the love of Christ; it is becoming that culture. Paul's suggestion to "become all things" was never behavioral in its intent— reflecting culture in such a way that we have its values and ideas mirrored in our own values and beliefs. Paul's intent was to build bridges of understanding upon which the two parties could meet. It is one thing to reach out to porn stars; it is another to embrace pornography.

Much of this flows from our cultural insecurities. We want to be accepted by culture, not simply because we want a hearing, but

because we long for cultural standing. In our efforts to distance ourselves from such enterprises as the Moral Majority, we seem fixated
on fitting in—and not just fitting in, but being seen as just as "hip"
as the next person. We have seemed to succumb to what some have
called the "celebrification" of culture—an awkward term, perhaps,
but like "industrialization" and "bureaucratization," it speaks to a
broad and historical trend: the increasing centrality of celebrities
to the culture. Movie and television stars, professional athletes and
musicians, business moguls and journalists have captured our attention as never before. Joseph Epstein writes that "a received opinion
about America in the early twenty-first century is that our culture
values only two things: money and celebrity."[5] From this, celebrities
have become our cultural commentators, charity spokespersons, role
models, and political candidates. They have become the arbiters of
taste, morality, and public opinion. Richard Schickel, who has written for *Time* magazine since 1972, reflects, "No issue or idea in our
culture can gain any traction with the general population unless it
has celebrity names attached to it."[6]

As a result, there is a seduction to move from building bridges in
and through such a celebrity culture to reach the world, to building
bridges in and through celebrity culture in order to be *accepted* by
the world—or to become celebrities ourselves. The cultural goal often
seems to be to get *in* the culture rather than remain on its outskirts,
leading some Christians to cling to Bono more than Bonhoeffer. Playing off the many motivational posters, one tongue-in-cheek blogger
phrased it, "Cultural Awareness: Following Bono to the Pub, to the
Concert, and to the Uttermost Parts of the Earth."[7]

No, an Acts 17 approach is not about reflecting culture; it is about
seeing America as the mission field. As an Episcopalian priest from
South Carolina recently offered, "A couple came into my office once
with a yellow pad of their teenage son's questions. One of them was:
'What is that guy doing hanging up there on the plus sign?'"

It's time we tell him.

☑ PART 2

6

Making Cars

This may be the most paradigm-shifting chapter in the book. Here's the essence of what I want to say: It used to be 130, but now it's 108.

As in the fact that the median worship attendance at a typical congregation has declined—again—from 130 to 108. According to Faith Communities Today, a Hartford Seminary study, the percentage of congregations with an average weekly worship attendance of one hundred or fewer moved from 42 percent to 49 percent. More than a quarter of all congregations had fifty or fewer people in attendance.[1]

And the megachurches, defined as congregations with two thousand or more weekly attendees? While the number doubled, they make up only 0.5 percent of all congregations. As David Roozen, author of the report "A Decade of Change in American Congregations, 2000–2010" and director of the Hartford Institute for Religion Research notes, "While it is true that the number of megachurches roughly doubled during the decade . . . and they are attracting an ever bigger slice of the religious attender pie, it is a bigger slice of a shrinking pie."[2]

Now, let's state the obvious: attendance is far from being the only metric that matters. Much has been said about the church's true effectiveness being much more than butts, bricks, and bucks (attendance, buildings, and giving). The greater question is what is happening to those people, and the greatest question is whether God is being glorified through the church as both community and mission.

Yet attendance does matter. The Great Commission has teeth; either you are reaching people for Christ or you are not. If you are reaching people, you'll grow numerically; if you're not, you won't.

So a number like 108 is concerning. But that isn't why this chapter is so important. It's because of the answer to a single question: Why is it so low?

The most glaring reason, and most indicting, is simple. When we think about growth, we are not thinking about *conversion growth*. We are thinking about *biological growth*, *transfer growth*, or perhaps *prodigal growth*. Until we think about conversion growth as the way to grow our churches, we won't make a dent in the fastest-growing religious demographic of our day.

Biological growth occurs when a child of existing believers with ties to a church comes to faith in Christ through his or her involvement in the church. Essentially, this is winning your own. For example, in the southern state of Kerala, India, where Catholics have long been a large minority group, church authorities believe the state's overall Christian population could drop to 17 percent this year, down from 19.5 percent in 1991. Worried about their dwindling numbers, the Roman Catholic Church in southern India announced a campaign to increase attendance by asking its flock to have more babies. It even went so far as to offer free schooling, medical care, and even cash bonuses for large families.[3]

Another way of growing is *transfer growth*. This takes place when a Christian moves into a new area and chooses to join a church, or when a locally churched Christian makes the decision to move to another church home. Such a person does not come to a church as a nonbeliever, nor does this person come from an unchurched background. At most, he or she is temporarily unchurched due to relocation or some other life issue. This type of growth, then, results from nothing more than the migration of existing believers. Translation: sheep swapping.

I recall many years ago reading an article about a large church that was experiencing financial difficulty. When asked why the church was stalled in its growth, the pastor replied that when they started, they were the only evangelical church around. Now there were several good

Bible-teaching churches. So people had a choice. That is why, he said, they weren't growing.

Even when churches see evidence of reaching the unchurched or marking high numbers of baptisms, it is often *prodigal growth*. A prodigal is someone without a recent church background or church involvement. This person previously embraced Christian beliefs and, in some cases, maintained a certain level of spirituality. For one reason or another, however, this person left the church and may have lived his or her life outside Christ's leadership. At the very least, a prodigal has certainly left the life of Christian community. Prodigal growth occurs when such a person returns to the church. Renewal and rededication may take place as part of the return and, at times, even rebaptism.

But missing in so many churches' thinking is *conversion growth*. This type of growth occurs when a church reaches a non-Christian. Consciously or not, such a person has never accepted the truth and claims of Christianity. Growing through conversion is reaching a person who has not entered into a life-changing, personal relationship with Christ as Savior and Lord.

If this emphasis doesn't change, small churches will keep getting smaller; big churches will keep attracting larger numbers of the already

---

Types of Church Growth

Biological Growth: when a child of existing believers with ties to a church comes to faith in Christ through his or her involvement in the church; aka winning your own

Transfer Growth: when a Christian moves into an area and chooses to join a church, or when a locally churched Christian decides to move to another church home; aka sheep swapping

Prodigal Growth: when someone who previously embraced Christian beliefs but then lived their life outside of Christ's leadership, returns to the church

Conversion Growth: when the church grows by reaching a person who has not entered into a life-changing, personal relationship with Christ as Savior and Lord

convinced (often at the expense of the smaller churches); the Christian population as a whole will remain in decline; and the *nones* will remain *nothing*.

Car Assembly Line

Think about a car assembly line. At the beginning of the line are the raw materials and parts needed to make a car: wire, engine, tires, chassis. Then, as those materials progress down the assembly line, a car is made. At the end of the line, the vehicle is rolled off for service (see figure 6.1).

Figure 6.1 Car Assembly Line

The dilemma is that many churches are specializing in one short segment of the assembly line (see figure 6.2). There is no effort to collect the raw material needed to build cars, and there is little effort to roll finished cars off the line for actual service and use on the road. The mission of these churches seems to be simply to keep new cars that have already been built well-tuned and polished for the showroom floor.

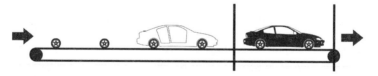

Figure 6.2 Car Assembly

This brings a foundational challenge on two levels. First, for the mission to be pursued, existing Christians must die to themselves for the sake of the cause. No longer can the mission be about us—it must be about those who have yet to darken our doorsteps.

But there's a second challenge that this brings to bear. If our mission is going to be the Great Commission, it will force us to grapple with the difficulties of the task. The mission cannot be simply to keep Christians happy and growing. Nor can it be about attempting to lure believers from other churches by having glitzier services and better programs. Our mission will actually have to target the *nones*.

Think of it this way: It is one thing to try to convince people wanting to fly from Charlotte to Atlanta to consider using Delta's services over US Airways. It is another thing altogether to get someone on board who has no desire to fly. Switching airlines would be akin to transfer growth—attracting the already convinced to your church. But getting someone averse to flying to step into the concourse, much less walk down the boarding ramp, is something altogether different. That's conversion growth.

I've often told people that if Meck had been focused on transfer growth, we would be much, much larger than we are now. Transfer growth is so much easier. These people want to fly! They are just looking for the best airline: best service, best seats, best flight times, best flight attendants, best pilots, best price. They are making a consumer decision; but make no mistake, they are ready to buy.

Conversion growth is much, much tougher. These are people who don't even like airports. And getting them past security, through the concourse, down the ramp, and into seat 15C? That's difficult. But *understandably* difficult, at least if you put yourself in the shoes of a *none*.

Learning from CarMax

I hate buying cars. I hate how the sales staff waits like vultures out front, descending on you before you even get out of your car. I hate how they push to get information about you—what you want to spend, are you going to trade in anything—all going into a plan to "work" you. I hate how they steer you away from what you really want to what they are trying to "move." I hate how hard it is to get straight answers. I hate how pushy they are to get you to decide then and there and won't let you walk away without getting as much contact information as possible. I hate haggling over a price: the back and forth, the mind games, and the manipulation. I hate having to bone up on the car's actual price, being coy about whether I'm going to trade in anything, and getting my guard up about the second salesperson who poses as a finance person but only wants to sell me more add-ons.

Did I mention I hate buying cars? So I didn't. For a long time. As in "two cars with over 200,000 miles each" long time. But at some point, life—and mileage—catches up. So I broke down and bought a car. Ready for a surprise? After my experience, I am actually looking forward to going back and, when needed, doing it again.

Why? Because of CarMax. (No, I don't work for them, get kick-backs, have family involved, or own stock.) Their slogan is simple: "The way car buying should be." And they're right. They have changed my entire attitude toward buying cars because they gave me an entirely different experience.

I could skip the lot, go online, and select exactly what I wanted in a car—type, mileage, price, features. Then a search engine showed me all the cars that fit my parameters. There was a no-haggle policy about the sticker price. The idea was simple: they set what they felt was a reasonable and competitive price, but there were no negotiating games. I could explore financing through the site, and if so desired, I could have it completed online before I went to the lot. The specific car I selected was ready for me to test drive when I arrived on the lot, even if it meant getting it there from fifty miles away. There was no bait and switch when I arrived or pressure to look at other cars. Because of the online process, when I bought the car, they even had my tags ready.

So a reluctant, even hostile customer became a raving fan. All it took was a different *process*. Same transaction, same product, same goal, but a radically different *experience*.

Now think about someone interested in exploring the Christian faith through a church. Yes, like me with a car, there will be times when even the most reluctant *nones* will find themselves walking through the doors. Whether because of a cultural event such as Easter or Christmas Eve, a milestone in life like the birth of a baby, a marriage, the loss of a loved one, or the invitation of a friend; even the most entrenched *nones* can find themselves in a church.

But let's face it. *They dread it.* As we've seen, many people are open to God but hate church. They hate having to dress up on a Sunday morning. They hate having to listen to music that is outdated, poorly performed, or just weird (what's up with building an Ebeneezer?). They hate feeling hit on for money, being assaulted by the ten-week sermon series titled "Tithe or Burn," or being forced to stare at a thermometer on the wall charting the latest fund drive. They hate being recognized as a first-time visitor, being made to stand out and feel more conspicuous than they already do, and then being forced to share contact information they aren't ready to give. They hate pushy, plastic, preachy types who say the word *God* as if it has three syllables. They hate being bored out of their skull for an hour or more. They hate feeling judged and being looked down on for their lack of regular attendance. They hate not knowing when to stand, when to sit, and what to recite.

They hate—*the experience.* But they don't hate God, just like I didn't hate new cars. I actually wanted a new car, just like many people truly want a relationship with God. So perhaps the first thing to consider for the mission, and the death of self involved in it, is a new way of doing church. Not a different product, as some mistakenly assume. It's not about watering things down, airbrushing out the tough parts on sin and repentance, or capitulating to cultural mores. After all, I didn't want a moped.

Just a new way of *doing* church, and doing it along the lines of what CarMax apparently did. Namely, listening to customers and finding out what it is they hate about the experience. No, not letting surveys create a consumer-driven theology or anything else that would compromise the gospel. But simply letting the feedback speak to the *experience* of attending—an experience that is often mired in practices, manners, and methods that can create an alienating and off-putting experience.

So is that all it takes for a new emphasis on conversion growth to take hold? No. The CarMax idea is simply suggestive of the kinds of changes that may need to be considered if you want to reach outsiders. The real paradigm shift is internal. It's how you *felt* about my CarMax example.

Spiritual Narcissism

The names say it all: YouTube, MySpace. And of course, the *i*'s: iPod, iTunes, iMac, and iPhone.[4] Each year *Time* magazine selects a "Person of the Year" who is the individual most central to current history and culture—filled in the past with presidents, dictators, business moguls, and religious leaders. When they searched for the person of the year for 2006, they made a selection that had never been made before: the word *You* on a mylar mirror so that the reader could see his or her reflection. If there is a theme to our day, it is: "It's all about me." Tom Wolfe had earlier labeled the 1970s the "Me Decade." In her book *Generation Me*, Jean M. Twenge writes that compared to today's generation, "They were posers."[5]

"Narcissus" by Leonardo da Vinci

In Greek mythology, Narcissus is the character who, on passing his reflection in the water, became so enamored with himself that he devoted the rest of his life to his own reflection. From this we get our term *narcissism*, the preoccupation with self. The value of narcissism is the classic "I, me, mine" mentality that places personal pleasure and fulfillment at the forefront of concerns. Historian Christopher Lasch went so far as to christen ours "the culture of narcissism," saying that this is the new religion—a religion in which we don't actually want religion proper but instead, personal therapy.[6] And it is just this spirit that has invaded our thinking and gone to war against the church.

Eavesdrop, for a moment, on our rhetoric: "I want to go where I'm fed"—not where we can learn to feed ourselves, much less feed others. "I need to be ministered to"—as if ministry in the life of the Christ follower is something that happens to us instead of something we make happen through us for others. We walk out of a worship service and say, "I didn't get anything out of it," as if its purpose is our edification instead of our worship of God.

Such a consumer mindset only looks at the church in terms of how it caters to specific felt needs. This from a people whose Savior said, "[I] did not come to be served, but to serve, and to give [my] life as a ransom for many" (Matt. 20:28). A Savior who said, "Anyone who wants to be first must be the very last" (Mark 9:35). A Savior who said, "Whoever wants to become great among you must be your servant" (Matt. 20:26). A Savior who said to the Father, "Not my will, but yours" (Luke 22:42). Yet a *spiritual* narcissism has invaded our thinking to the point that the individual needs and desires of the believer have become the center of attention. And it is precisely this spirit that is turning us away from conversion growth and doing whatever it may take to reach the *nones*.

Consider the first two questions any organization must ask itself, courtesy of management expert Peter Drucker: (1) What is our mission? (2) Who is our customer?[7] The second of these involves crass language, I know, for any church. But let's consider these questions for a moment.

First, what is our mission? Few would deny that it is to seek and save the lost. So clear were our marching orders from Jesus in this regard that the passage in which he gives us our mission is called the "Great Commission." So how can we have a mission other than the one Christ entrusted to us as the church? Yes, the Great Commission also involves discipleship, but we cannot pursue discipleship apart from having someone to disciple. If you never reach anyone for Christ, who, exactly, will you be discipling? Evangelism must be in the vanguard, which is why Jesus says we are to first make disciples and *then* teach them to obey everything he commanded.

From this comes the second question: Who, then, is our primary customer? The answer is inescapable. If our mission is to seek and save (and then disciple) the lost, then our customer is the one who is lost. Yet here is the point of the breakdown. Most churches have as their primary focus reaching and then serving the already convinced. So the mission isn't making disciples but rather caring for them. From this, services rendered to the believer become paramount. Existing Christians are the customer in a consumer-driven mission. As a result, conversion growth is given lip service, while biological growth and transfer growth become the defining reality.

The Truth about (Many) Christians and Evangelism

Here is the uncomfortable truth. Almost everybody who follows Christ, and almost every gathering of those Christ followers constituting a church, says the same thing: "We want to reach the world for Christ." Yet most don't do it. So where's the breakdown?

It's not strategy. There are vast numbers of churches who are successfully penetrating the culture of the *nones*, growing through conversion growth, and who willingly offer their tried-and-true strategies to any and all who wish to learn.

It's not theology. As mentioned earlier, almost every Christian church has evangelism as part of its core values and integral to their mission statement.

It's not the new generation of leadership. Most young leaders got into the game to see a lost world won to Christ. They are sold out and ready to rock.

It's not the new generation of Christians. If you want to meet an evangelistic animal, spend time with a new believer. They are, in the best sense of the word, shameless with enthusiasm.

So what *is* the problem?

Jesus knew. When challenged about his own missional emphasis toward those on the outside of faith, he responded: "Who needs a doctor: the healthy or the sick? Go figure out what this Scripture means: 'I'm after mercy, not religion.' I'm here to invite outsiders, not coddle insiders" (Matt. 9:12–13 Message).

The problem? Seemingly long-term insiders. Countless leaders and members of churches have given in to a Christian consumerism. They embrace a mentality that gives ample rhetorical support to evangelistic intent but resists violently at the point of implementation because—at the point of actually *doing* it—it *costs* them. In other words, scratch the surface of a sacrificial, pick-up-your-cross, to-die-is-gain, eat-my-flesh and drink-my-blood Christian, and you find an it's-all-about-me, spiritually narcissistic, turned-inward, meet-my-needs, feed-me consumer.

Again, listen to how we talk: Of course I want to reach lost people,

but I'm not going to let the music change

but I'm not going to lead a capital campaign to raise the money

but I'm not going to park far away

but I'm not going to risk stirring things up right now in the church

but I'm not going to attend at a different service time

but I'm not going to start a new church

but I'm not going to stand for the pastor dressing casually

but I'm not going to give money to launch a new site or relocate

but I'm not going to watch someone on a video

but I'm not going to put in fifty- or sixty-hour weeks

but I'm not going to let them start playing drums

but I'm not going to change how I preach

but I'm not going to give up my favorite seat

but I'm not going to turn things over to a bunch of twentysomethings

but I'm not going to attend on Saturday night

but I'm not going to . . .

You fill in the rest.

I'm not even suggesting this list is what a church *should* do. But it does betray our spirit. The problem with outreach today is that the very people who say they want unchurched people to come and find Jesus resist the most basic and elemental issues related to building a relationship with someone apart from Christ, then engaging in spiritual conversations, and then inviting them to an open, winsome, and compelling *front door* so they can come and see, come and hear, come and experience.

Why? Because it would call for sacrifice or inconvenience of some kind. A leader would have to work harder or invest in vision-casting and face potential opposition. Attendees would have to be part of a church that no longer exists solely to serve them but now serves those who have yet to enter the doors. This means that evangelism is fine in theory but not in practice, because in practice evangelism almost always involves death-to-self—the complete anticonsumer state of mind.

So can we change? Sure. But only when we look in the mirror and own the truth about our consumerism: we say we want them in heaven—but we act like they can go to hell.

Questions for Discussion and Reflection

1. Church membership continues to decline. Last Sunday more than a quarter of all congregations had fewer than fifty people in attendance. What do you think is contributing to the sustained drop?

2. When growth is discussed, it often doesn't center around conversion growth—growth coming from those previously unchurched or nonbelievers. Does your church distinguish between transfer and conversion growth? On which do you put more emphasis?

3. If we think about disciples of Christ as being on a car assembly line, we need to shift our focus from the "finished product" to the "raw materials," meaning the unchurched who are far from Christ. Is part of your mission, personally and in your church, to reach the *nones* and help them down the assembly line?

4. In the CarMax example, we saw someone who hates buying cars be converted into a raving fan. But just like someone who finds himself or herself in need of a new car, a *none* will sometimes

find himself or herself in a church. If a *none* sat in your church this weekend, how would he or she interpret the experience?

5. Spiritual narcissism has crept into American Christianity, where the needs of the believer have become the center of attention. Think carefully about your own church and its programs, its weekend services, and how it spends its energy and money. Does it reflect a spiritual narcissism or a missional strategy to reach those like the *nones*?

6. "We want to seek and save the lost" is a common thing to say in church, but there's far more to this than simply uttering the phrase. It takes a willingness to change music, shift focus, reshape ministries, and inconvenience believers. Do your actions as a church affirm your intentions to seek and save the lost? If not, what's holding you back?

7. Read this statement about the lost: "We say we want them in heaven—but we act like they can go to hell." How did you feel? Did it convict you? Were you offended? And if so, why do you think you were?

7

If You Build It, They Won't Come

Another one came this past week. A flyer arrived in my mailbox from a new church plant, promising me relevant and practical messages, contemporary "urban" music, and great coffee. The idea behind the mailer seemed to be, "If you build it, they will come." Or more to the point, "If you offer it, they will come." Meaning that if you spruce church up a bit musically and stylistically, and if the unchurched are informed, those same unchurched people will suddenly stream in your doors and fill your seats.

No, they won't.

Not if they are truly unchurched, part of the growing number of religious *nones* that make up our modern milieu. Yes, it worked in the movie *Field of Dreams*. A man built a baseball diamond in the middle of a cornfield having been promised, "If you build it, he will come"—meaning Shoeless Joe Jackson and other members of the 1919 Chicago White Sox. Eventually crowds of people do come to watch baseball there. Sounds strange, but it's a fun film.

But don't ever think that's all there is to reaching an unchurched person who isn't even looking for a defined faith, much less a church. It's a subtle and enticing temptation. All we have to do is encourage casual dress, offer Starbucks coffee, play rock music, and then deliver a "felt needs" message in a style similar to the popular speakers of the day, and we will automatically grow. And if you want to guarantee your growth comes from a younger demographic, just throw in skinny jeans, designer T-shirts, and a noticeable tattoo. It will instantly turn the most middle-aged pastor into a Millennial magnet.

The only problem is that it isn't true. Yet it persists as one of the great urban legends of the ecclesiastical world.

Some will say, "But wait. I know of a new church plant that went uber-contemporary, and they exploded in growth!" Yes, I know of several too. But look hard at those churches. How much of their growth is transfer growth and how much is truly conversion growth? And even if they claim a high number of baptisms, who are they baptizing? In many cases, even the baptism numbers are those rededicating their life (rebaptisms) or Presbyterians getting dunked as adults. Or it's kids and teenagers—meaning, reaping the work of already existing Christian families.

One of the least publicized research projects of the 1990s, but easily one of the most significant, discovered that more than 60 percent of adults baptized in Southern Baptist churches that year had been baptized before. And of those who were rebaptized, nearly 40 percent were receiving their second immersion in a Southern Baptist church. Overall, rebaptisms of Southern Baptists accounted for one out of every five Southern Baptist baptisms.[1]

Hear my heart; I'm not putting down such churches. I just want to make sure we understand our models. And specifically, that if we want to be a church for the unchurched—which today increasingly means a church of the *nones*—we understand what that means. Because even if a contemporary church plant grows rapidly from the unchurched, and many do, those people didn't come first and foremost because it was contemporary.

Let's go back to the mailer I received. It promised contemporary music, casual dress, and good coffee.

Stop. Think.

People already have those things. They do not need to go to church to find them. If they want Starbucks, they'll go to Starbucks; if they want to hear contemporary music, they have iTunes and their iPod. They may appreciate those things once they attend, but it is not what will *get* them to attend. This approach may have worked back in the 1980s and '90s, but that was because the typical unchurched person was a baby boomer who had been raised in a church and was just starting to have kids. They had the memory and the experience; once they had kids, they actually *wanted* to find a church. When churches took down the cultural barriers associated with attending (eliminating stuffiness, boredom, irrelevance, empty ritual, outdated music), boomers *were* attracted. And yes, back then if you built it, they came.

But this is no longer our world, and it hasn't been for quite some time. Think of it this way: In today's paper, there were probably dozens of ads for new cars. In fact, there was probably an entire section devoted to nothing but car ads. If you read the paper, did you notice them? It's doubtful—unless you are in the market for a car. (These days, it's doubtful you even read a newspaper—but let's play this out.) If you're not in the market for a car, it doesn't matter to you if a dealer is having a sale, promises a rebate, has an on-site radio broadcast, hangs out balloons, says they're better than everyone else, promises that they will be different and not harass you or make you bargain over the price, or sends you a brochure or an email.

Why? You're not in the market for a car.

It's amazing the degree to which outreach strategies rest on a single, deeply flawed premise that *people want what you have to offer.* More often than not, they don't.

As uber-marketer Seth Godin notes, "The portion of the population that haven't bought from you . . . is not waiting for a better mousetrap. They're not busy considering a, b and c and then waiting for d. No, they're not in the market. . . . As a result, smart marketers don't market to this audience by saying, 'hey ours is better than theirs!'"[2]

It's no different with a church. The vast majority of those who are unchurched are not actively seeking a church home. Further, they are divorced from seeing it as a need in their life, even when they are open to and interested in spiritual things. They no longer tie their spiritual interest and longing to the need to find a particular faith, much less a particular church. If anything, they are antichurch.

So direct mail efforts that offer casual dress and Starbucks coffee, contemporary music and practical messages, are offering cars to those who aren't in the market for a car. These promos are simply positioning themselves as an alternative to other churches when the people in question are not interested in church at all. Godin is spot-on when he writes, "No, they won't respond to a better-than-them pitch. Instead, they're much more likely to respond to a new statement of their problem and a new statement of the solution. Don't ask them to announce that they were wrong when they decided that they didn't need a tablet, a survival kit or an anti-impotence drug. Instead, make it easy for them to make a new decision based on new information."[3]

Rethinking Evangelism

Picture an imaginary scale from 1 to 10. On the left end of the scale, at the 1, we have someone who is completely divorced from a relationship with or knowledge of Christ. On the other end of the scale, at the 10, is that point in time when the spiritual journey of an individual results in coming to saving faith in and knowledge of Christ. I know, this is a crude and overly simplistic scale, but let me try to illustrate the point.

1	10
No relationship with Christ	Saving faith in Christ

Let's begin by using this scale to evaluate the typical unchurched person of the past. Speaking in broad terms, where on the scale would such a person living in the United States in 1960 have been?

Few would deny that the typical unchurched person of that time was far from a *none*. More than likely their spiritual résumé included

an acceptance of the deity of Christ
a belief that truth exists and that the Bible is trustworthy
a positive image of the church and its leaders
a church background and experience that was relatively healthy
a foundational knowledge of the essential truths of the Christian faith
a built-in sense of guilt or conviction that kicked in when he or she violated the basic tenets of the Judeo-Christian value system

Whew!
So on a scale of 1 to 10, this person can be placed at 8.

1	8	10
No relationship with Christ	Accepts basic Christian beliefs	Saving faith in Christ

The top evangelistic strategies of 1960—revivals, door-to-door visitation, Sunday school, and busing—were well oriented to this context. For example, revivals were productive because people who needed Christ would actually attend them due to the cultural pressure to be present. Door-to-door visitation was effective because people opened their doors to church folk and gladly invited them into their home. Regardless of a person's spiritual convictions, failure to have done so would have been considered rude.

Sunday school was evangelistically fruitful because individuals were not too intimidated to begin their exploration of a church through a small group experience. Sunday school enrollment campaigns also benefited from the cultural pressure to open one's door, the positive image of the church, and the built-in sense of conviction that resulted from not being involved in church. Once enrolled, there was a strong sense of obligation to attend; it was, after all, the church.

And bus ministries? They were supported by parents who willingly allowed their children to board a vehicle driven by a stranger, be transported to some building in another part of the city for a religious event to be implemented by more strangers, and then be returned to them later that day.

Yeah, right. But it was effective because that is precisely how it worked.

With each of these efforts (because unchurched people were already at an 8 on the scale), a one-time, cold-call presentation of the gospel was effective. After all, they did not need to move very far up the line—just from an 8 to a 10. All it took was a bump.

One of the most pressing questions for the church in today's world is this: Are the conditions and attitudes that created such a successful context for those strategies still in place today? Are the people we are trying to reach today the same as they were in 1960?

The answer is no. Today the typical unchurched person is not simply unchurched, but as charted earlier, more than likely he or she is in the *none* category.

A few years ago, sensing the sea change that was afoot, I began speaking of something I called (borrowing from C. S. Lewis) "The Great Divorce." I was attempting to describe a separation between spiritual longing and desire and the embrace of a particular religious faith. It wasn't that people were far away from Christ and his church in their life and knowledge; instead, they no longer saw their spiritual desire and search as involving the discovery of a faith or religion. There were too many roads to God, so they were no longer even looking for a road. If the current malaise was simply about belief in Christianity as "the way," our challenge would be creating deeper levels of understanding. If the impasse involved doubt that Christianity is the way, that would take an effort toward convincing. Today, people reject that there's even a way, so the challenge is to show that there is even a need for Christianity itself.

So where does the contemporary unchurched person rest on our imaginary scale? One could theorize that he or she is best placed at a 3.

1	3		10
No relationship with Christ	The *nones*		Saving faith in Christ

Now reflect on the implications this may have on traditional evangelistic approaches. In a day when reports of child molestation and sexual abuse by religious leaders make headlines and when confidence in religious leadership is so low, it is highly doubtful that many parents will allow their children to participate in a traditional bus ministry. Door-to-door visitation of any kind has been declared unlawful in many areas and impossible in the ever-growing number of closed, guarded, gated communities. More to the point, few people today enjoy an unannounced visitor knocking on their door and will not risk opening it to a stranger. Revivals no longer have the cultural support they once enjoyed as a community event, and as a result, they have very few non-Christians in attendance. Church members are finding that many people are too intimidated to begin their spiritual journey with a small group experience such as Sunday school and that traditional enrollment campaigns suffer for the same reasons as door-to-door visitation.

Even if a Christian *does* get a foot in the door or manages to get a friend to a revival, the impact of a one-time, cold-call type presentation is greatly diminished because the typical nonbeliever is no longer at an 8 on the scale. It takes time for someone to move up the scale. And while there are clearly some Saul-to-Paul experiences, they are the exceptions, not the rule.

It is time to rethink evangelism, and that begins with capturing a new understanding of evangelism—one that sees evangelism as both process and event.

Evangelism as Process and Event

In my relationship with my wife, Susan, there was a process of dating and courtship that preceded the actual event of our marriage. It is rare for people to become engaged, much less get married, on their first date.

It is no different with Christ. When someone comes to saving faith in Christ, there is both an adoption process and an actual decision event. Yet for the last several decades, evangelism capitalized on a unique state of affairs, namely a culture filled with people who were relatively advanced in their spiritual knowledge and, as a result, able to quickly and responsibly consider the event of accepting Christ as Savior and Lord.

In light of today's realities, there must be fresh attention paid to the *process* that leads people to the event of salvation. The goal is not simply knowing how to articulate the means of coming to Christ (the 10 moment); it is learning how to facilitate and enable the person to progress from a 3 to a 7 or 8, where he or she is able to even *consider* accepting Christ in a responsible fashion.

When I was in elementary school, one of my teachers brought an incubator to class. We learned that an incubator maintains the kind of environment that is necessary for the birth of a baby chick. If it became too cold for the eggs, the baby bird inside the egg would die. In order for the egg to hatch, there had to be a certain degree of warmth. When it comes to evangelism, the efforts of the church need to be like an incubator. Every approach, every program, every service furnishes a particular environment that will either serve the evangelistic process or hinder it.

Let's use our term *none* to represent a person who may be open to spiritual things but is at a 3 on the scale. This person is in desperate need of someone or something to facilitate the process of moving him or her up the line toward being able to even consider the life and message of Christ. The following types of environments are among those that a church can present.

None Hostile

The first environment a church can manifest is *none hostile*. A church can be openly antagonistic toward *nones* who may venture in to attend its services.

Michelle was trapped in the demeaning world of prostitution, drug addiction, and alcoholism. Wanting to escape this life, Michelle disguised herself and hid from her pimp for several days while going through chemical withdrawal. She was discovered and dragged into the chambers of the raging man, where she was beaten until unconscious while the other prostitutes watched and learned.

Next Michelle tried suicide—anything to escape the nightmare of her existence. A relative found her body, hours from death, and rushed her to the hospital, where her life was saved.

This time Michelle turned to the only place she could imagine there might be hope—a local church. She had no sense of self-worth. Used by men, rejected by the world, she turned to God's people. She knew she deserved punishment but hoped against hope that she might find mercy. Halfway through the church service, the pastor recognized her from her life on the street. Before the entire congregation he pointed her out and then lectured her for defiling the house of God with her filthy presence. Then he ordered her out.[4]

An extreme case? Perhaps. But it is all too common in lesser forms.

Kristina and her roommate decided to go to church because they had hit on some rough times. Kristina's roommate had become pregnant outside of marriage. They decided to search a little deeper for purpose and meaning. High on their list for investigation was Christianity.

They decided to try a church near their apartment. They went, attended faithfully, and tried to build some relationships. They both wanted to turn from the lifestyles they had been living and seek God. After just a few weeks, however, it became known in the church

Church Environments toward *Nones*

None Hostile: openly antagonistic toward *nones* who venture in

None Indifferent: not hostile, but apathetic and unwilling to answer *nones'* questions

None Hopeful: want to see the *nones* reach Christ, but unwilling to change their environment

None Sensitive: want to reach *nones*, and willing to change the environment, but still primarily cater to the already convinced

None Targeted: church members place a high priority on the needs of *nones* and make every effort to remove any and all barriers that may impede the exploration process

No Man's Land: not being targeted enough to reach the unchurched, but being too targeted to the unchurched for the churched

---

that the baby carried by Kristina's roommate was conceived out of wedlock. Suddenly people wouldn't sit by them and stopped talking whenever they approached. No one smiled at them when they entered the church. It wasn't long before the pastor asked them not to return because of the nature of their situation. As you can imagine, Kristina and her roommate never wanted to darken the doorstep of a church again.

The pastor's explanation? "You're just not our type."

None Indifferent

A second environment can be termed *none indifferent*. This church climate is not hostile but merely apathetic. The questions, concerns, and exploration process of a person who may be at a 3 on the scale and is interested in moving up the line are simply overlooked.

While in New England for a speaking engagement, I recall meeting a pastor of a Baptist church who shared his frustrations regarding the growth of his church. I asked him what he thought the problem was and he responded, "Well, there just aren't any more Baptists in my area." Cultivating an atmosphere for someone who was not a

Baptist, much less a Christian, had never entered his mind. He was not hostile to those outside the church; he was just oblivious to them.

None Hopeful

A church that creates a *none hopeful* environment wants to see *nones* come and meet Christ, but they have never thought about the nature of the church's climate. Altar calls are extended with great hope and fervor, revivals are held, Sunday school campaigns are enacted, but the warmth of the incubator has not been adjusted. The internal environment has not been changed for years, and as a result, nothing has been done that will effectively bring in *nones*, much less serve their pilgrimage toward Christ. This type of environment is like a fishing expedition in which people put bait on a hook, place it in the middle of the boat's deck, and then join hands to pray for the fish to jump in and grab the hook.

None Sensitive

A fourth environment a church can offer is *none sensitive*. This atmosphere exhibits some concrete efforts to draw and encourage the *nones*. While the overall orientation of the church is still directed toward the growth and maturation of the *already convinced*, the thermostat has clearly been adjusted to allow all eggs to receive some of the warmth and care they need in order to hatch.

None Targeted

The fifth atmospheric category is best termed *none targeted*. This is preferable to being *none driven*, which would mistakenly intimate that the whim of the *nones* is what determines the theology and direction of the church. In truth, a *none-targeted* environment is one in which church members place a high priority on the needs of the *nones* and, like CarMax in the previous chapter, make every effort to remove any and all barriers that could impede the exploration process. Every barrier, that is, except the scandal of the cross. This is not about an abandonment of orthodoxy in an effort to cater to the sensibilities of those alien to the Christian faith. A *none-targeted* climate is just that—targeted on facilitating the process of evangelizing *nones*. The growth and maturation of believers is certainly cared for, but there is a conscious attempt to be an evangelistic incubator that is set at just the right temperature in regard to the front door or entry points of the church.

But there is still one more environment, and it is arguably the most subtle of all.

No Man's Land

I grew up with Wheaties, the cereal known as the "Breakfast of Champions." You knew an athlete had arrived on the cultural scene if his or her picture landed on the front of one of its boxes. But Wheaties has fallen onto hard times of late. There are many reasons for this, but industry insiders say that the heart of the matter is simple: Wheaties is in *no man's land*.

That's my terminology, but here's what the pundits are saying: Wheaties isn't healthy enough for the Fiber One crowd, and it isn't unhealthy enough for the Frosted Flakes crowd. That's *no man's land*. By not positioning itself firmly in any camp—not quite the health food, not quite the junk food—it reaches no one.[5]

It's not just cereal that can fall into this category. The heart of *no man's land* for a church is not being targeted *enough* to reach the unchurched but being *too* targeted to the unchurched for the churched. Such churches are too tilted to those exploring the Christian faith to have their weekend services attract large numbers of traditionally minded, church-is-for-me believers, yet too caught in the cultural trappings of traditional church to attract explorers—or at least have their members feel comfortable inviting their unchurched friends.

Why is it so common for churches to find themselves in *no man's land*? It's because many churches get the surface issues of connecting with those outside the church but little more. They get the music, the dress, the style. Yet they don't go far enough in leading the church to have a missional heart to reach out to those outside the church and invite them in; and they don't have culturally informed and culturally sensitive messages and environments that address the questions and concerns of our day. In other words, they have style but not substance, décor but not decorum. They're trying to stand on Mars Hill with an Acts 17 vibe, but they're doing it with a Jerusalem/Acts 2 DNA. So they end up reaching neither group.

They know about Mars Hill, talk about Mars Hill, even yearn for Mars Hill; but they don't really know, in an intuitive sense, how to *stand* on Mars Hill. They are cultural critics, even cultural students, but not cultural *apologists*. A real Mars Hill person could spend ten minutes in their church service and see a mindset oriented toward those already convinced of Jerusalem playing out all over the place.

You pick where your church should stand—Mars Hill or Jerusalem. Of course I would argue for Mars Hill. But whatever you do, there's one place you don't want to find yourself: *no man's land*.

Questions for Discussion and Reflection

1. Have you fallen into the trap of "if you build it, they will come"?
2. If so, it may stem from a false belief that people want what you are *selling*. More often than not, they don't. They don't want religion—especially not the caustic brand of Christianity they think is being offered. Are you assuming people want what you have to offer? Are you providing something they can already get elsewhere?
3. Are the conditions and attitudes of the religiously unaffiliated the same today as they were in the 1960s? Does your outreach strategy look any different than that of a church in the 1960s?
4. An important thing to remember about evangelism is that it takes time, especially when those outside the faith are openly hostile to it. Is your church paying attention to the process leading up to the event of salvation? What would that even look like?
5. This chapter detailed several different church environments from the perspective of the *nones*. If you had to pick one to describe your church, which would it be: *none* hostile, *none* indifferent, *none* hopeful, *none* sensitive, *none* targeted, or *no man's land*?
6. Why did you rate it that way?
7. Which would you like to be?
8. What strategic steps do you need to take to get to that environment?

8

The Importance of Cause

The rise of the *nones* calls for not only a renewed commitment to conversion growth and a rethinking of evangelism as both process and event, but also a new understanding of strategic effectiveness. Simply put, there has been a seismic shift in outreach that few church leaders are understanding, much less pursuing.

From the 1950s to the 1980s, the vanguard of evangelistic outreach was *direct proclamation* of the gospel. Whether the crusades of Billy Graham or the creative approach of Willow Creek Community Church, presentation led the way. This resulted in the unchurched joining a community and eventually being discipled into participation with the cause of Christ.

From the 1990s thru the 2000s, *community* took the strategic lead. People wanted to belong before they believed. Skepticism was rampant, and trust had to be earned. Once enfolded into that community, Christ was often met in its midst. *Cause*, again, was the last to be manifest.

From the 2010s forward, *cause*—think campaigns to rescue girls from sex trafficking or food drives to end hunger—became the leading edge of our connection with a lost world, and specifically the *nones*, in terms of both arresting their attention and enlisting their participation in community and relationship. Consider the recent

Passion Conference in Georgia. What captured outside media attention was not the sixty thousand students in attendance, much less the
messages related to the Christian faith; what attracted the media was
their commitment to eradicate modern-day slavery—in a word: *cause*.
Then and only then did community come into play. After exploring
that community, Christ could be—and was—introduced.

As the Pew Forum's study reveals, the *nones* believe religious organizations are too concerned with money and power, rules and
politics. And many believe that religious institutions do very little
to help protect morality. Only 28 percent say that belonging to a
community of people with shared values and beliefs is important
to them. Yet they do believe that churches and other religious institutions benefit society by strengthening community and aiding
the poor. Three-quarters say religious organizations bring people
together and help strengthen community bonds (78 percent), and a
similar number say religious organizations play an important role
in helping the poor and needy (77 percent).[1] In other words, we may
have lost the opportunity to talk to them and do life with them, but
we haven't lost the opportunity to do good *to* them, *before* them,
and *with* them—good that will then open their ears and hearts to
the message of the gospel.

Think of this shift in terms of moving people through stages of
introduction:

1950s–1980s
> Unchurched → Christ → Community → Cause

1990s–2000s
> Unchurched → Community → Christ → Cause

2010s–
> Nones → Cause → Community → Christ

I know some of you will be uncomfortable seeing how far the message
of Christ is down the strategic line. It's not that the church should
bury the lede in terms of intentionally putting Christ at the end of

the line, and it's certainly not implying some kind of bait and switch. Remember, we're talking strategy. Leading with Billy Graham's simple, "The Bible says," was effective for people in a different place spiritually than most are today.

Reflect on the ground we've already covered. The more post-Christian a person is, the more evangelism must embrace not only event/proclamation, but also process *and* event/proclamation. Earlier models were almost entirely event/proclamation-oriented, such as revivals, crusades, or door-to-door visitation. This is only effective in an Acts 2, God-fearing Jews of Jerusalem context. Process models are needed in Acts 17, Mars Hill, *nones*/skeptical contexts.

The presentation of Christ must remain central to our thinking, to be sure. It would be tragic to buy a pair of shoes from Tom's Shoes as an act of social concern but not witness to Tom. That is the only reason we are even talking about strategy; the goal is to present Christ and him crucified. But is that where we start? On Mars Hill, the spiritual illiteracy was so deep that Paul had to begin with cultural touchstones, lead into creation, and work his way forward. It took him a while to get to Christ.

And community? It matters, but the average person has tastes of that already. Maybe not a particularly functional community, but people don't seem as drawn to it as they once were. Perhaps it is because of the lure and illusion of social media, or because they've simply given up on it, or because they have grown suspect of its authenticity in any place or form. Community does not seem to have the great attraction it once did. Instead, there has been a great seismic shift. Today it is *cause* that arrests the attention of the world.

That brings us to the challenges: first, to recognize the seismic shift and begin to strategize accordingly; second, to realize how difficult this will be. If *cause* is in the lead and *community* close behind, the church is at a deficit. In the minds of many, our causes have been mundane (let's raise money for a fellowship hall) or alienating (Moral Majority). And as mentioned in the chapter "Lawyers, Guns, and Money," being on the wrong side of *cause* can be as detrimental—if not more so—as not having a cause at all.

For example, a United Methodist minister who runs a Christian coffee shop in Dallas was interviewed on the rise of the *nones* by

National Public Radio. He offered the following lament on the immigration issue:

> If the church was known more for our efforts to welcome the stranger than keep them out, I think the church would have greater credibility with rising generations. For example, on immigration policies, we've taken the wrong stance on that, and they know. The thing is they're smart enough. A lot of them have grown up in the church and then rejected it. They've read the Scriptures that talk about the importance of welcoming the stranger; they've read the Scriptures about the importance of caring for the poor; and when they see that no longer on the lips of those who are in religious authority, they see that the God we present is bankrupt, and that we're theologically thin in our ability to even speak our own story.[2]

There is great irony in the challenge. Jesus wed mission and message together seamlessly, proclaiming the kingdom that had come while healing the leper and feeding the hungry. He mandated concern for the widow and orphan, the homeless and naked, the imprisoned and hungry while speaking of the bread of life and a home in heaven. In other words, we should have been nailing this all along.

But what is it we are after with *cause*? If we are attempting to be counter-cultural agents of change through the creation of the common good, what is the common good? Mark Galli, editor at *Christianity Today* magazine, has written that our goal is not cultural transformation as much as it is personal obedience and service. As has often been noted, neither Jesus nor Paul seemed particularly concerned about addressing the immediate and most obvious (to the people of that day) cultural challenges of the Roman Empire. Jesus did not seem as interested in altering that kingdom as much as he was in ushering in an altogether new one; and when questioned, he as much as told Pilate exactly that. We know we are to be witnesses; we are to make disciples; we are to do justice, love mercy, feed the hungry, and care for the widow and orphan. This is obviously far from pursuing a privatized faith. We know we are called to be present in culture as salt. That, of course, can and often should lead to transformation—but more to the point, it can lead to renewal.[3] But what does renewal mean?

Andy Crouch, in his book *Culture Making*, refers to it as the title suggests: the practice of *making* culture, drawing on the biblical ideas of *creation* and *cultivation*.[4] Too often, he writes, we have settled for condemning, critiquing, copying, or consuming culture. All have their place, but they pale in comparison to the deeper ideas of creation and cultivation. Sociologist James Davison Hunter argues similarly, maintaining that cultural transformation only occurs through cultural renewal, such as "compelling artistic and intellectual works produced by a movement of cultural visionaries and the networks they build." Once such visionaries gain a foothold in society, their words galvanize a culture.[5] Our tools for such an effort have never changed: prayer, evangelism, example, argument, action, and suffering.[6]

But again, the dilemma is that we too often do not know what *making* culture is supposed to *make*. We know to act, but where? We are willing to suffer, but for which cause? We are to embody faith, hope, and love, but to what end? As T. S. Eliot notes, "It is not enough simply to see the evil and injustice and suffering of this world, and precipitate oneself into action. What we must know, what only theology can tell us, is why these things are wrong. Otherwise, we may right some wrongs at the cost of creating new ones."[7] So what is the cultural target on the wall? Yes, God's kingdom, but what does the reign of that kingdom entail?

What actually constitutes *kingdom culture*? Truth, goodness, and beauty have been called the three fundamental values because the worth of anything can be exhaustively judged by reference to these three standards. Everything that *is* is related to whether it is true or false, good or evil, beautiful or ugly. Truth, goodness, and beauty constitute what it is that we are trying to achieve through our efforts to renew this culture as followers of Christ. But that simply begs the question: What are the true, the good, and the beautiful?

Here are some pictures that may help.[8]

The True

During a recent trip to Washington, DC, I met with a group of highly influential Christians involved in public policy, including lobbyists, lawyers in the Justice Department, and presidential appointees. To a person, they voiced two things: (1) a clear sense of calling to their role, and (2) a strong frustration that other followers of Christ were often critical about how they were pursuing that calling. Some Christians outside Washington insisted that the only appropriate way to be a Christian in Washington was to share Christ on every elevator, make speeches littered with Scripture on the congressional floor, and insist on biblical language in every policy. Instead, these Christians I met with expressed a desire for fellow believers to understand how their calling is rooted in the dynamics of common grace, finding its most effective expression in the appeal to natural law.

Common grace is grace that is extended to all human beings through God's general providence (see Matt. 5:45; Heb. 1:2–3; John 1:1–4). For example, consider the nurture of rain and sun and the resulting bounty of a harvest. This should not be confused with *prevenient grace*, meaning the specific grace that runs *before* (the meaning of the Latin *preveniens*) and enables a decision for Christ, affording individuals the ability to respond to God's call for salvation. Instead, common grace, writes theologian Stanley Grenz, "speaks of God's extension of favor to all people through providential care, regardless of whether or not they acknowledge and love God."[9]

And what has this to do with Christians in Washington and the creation of what is *true*? The Anglican scholar Philip Edgcumbe Hughes writes that "common grace is evident in the divine government or control of human society. It is true that human society is in a state of sinful fallenness. Were it not for the restraining hand of God, indeed, our world would long since have degenerated into a self-destructive chaos of iniquity, in which social order and community life would have been an impossibility."[10] For those who attempt to honor Christ

---

Common Grace vs. Prevenient Grace

Common Grace: grace that is extended to all human beings through God's general providence

Prevenient Grace: the specific grace that runs *before* (the meaning of the Latin *preveniens*) and enables a decision for Christ, affording individuals the ability to respond to God's call for salvation

within the nation's capital, it is the active participation in and work-ing for the extension of common grace that fills their waking hours. We should be glad for such commitment. As Charles Colson writes, "Understanding Christianity as a worldview is important not only for fulfilling the great commission but also for fulfilling the cultural commission—the call to create a culture under the lordship of Christ. God cares not only about redeeming souls but also about restoring his creation. He calls us to be agents not only of his saving grace but also of his common grace. Our job is not only to build up the church but also to build a society to the glory of God."[11]

And on what basis do they pursue this *common* grace? Most often through an appeal to natural law, such as the law of gravity, the prin-ciples of which can be found in nature itself. For those Christians engaged in public policy, natural law provides the basis on which an appeal to conscience about the good (and the evil) can be made. It is how a Christian in a secular setting can make an appeal to what is *right* among those who do not share a conviction that biblical reve-lation is a source of truth yet still will allow that Christian to lead them *to* that truth source. The appeal to natural law provided the foundation for the moral philosophy of Thomas Aquinas and, with important modifications, was employed by Luther and Calvin. More recently, the arguments of C. S. Lewis in *Mere Christianity* made ample use of this idea.

So rather than finding a model in Peter speaking to the God-fearing Jews in Jerusalem (Acts 2), those in Washington find a clearer model for their vocation in such Old Testament lives as Joseph, Daniel, and Esther. Such figures served public policy in very secular settings, working within the system in obedience to God, and through that obedience, they affected the system for God. This is renewing culture toward the *true*.

The Good

For over fifty years, Michael Haynes served as pastor of the his-toric Twelfth Baptist Church in the Roxbury district of downtown Boston. Twelfth Baptist Church is a direct descendant of the First

African Baptist Meeting House on Beacon Hill, founded in 1805. In 1840, a band of dissenters from the church felt led of the Holy Spirit to become involved in the Underground Railroad, an organized means of smuggling slaves from bondage in the South to freedom in the North. They became known as the Twelfth Baptist Church of Boston.

When I first met Michael, I asked him what he did. He said he was a pastor of a church. "Just a little church in Roxbury. That's my ministry. Just three or four city blocks." One of the first persons on those blocks that he had a chance to serve was a young man named Martin. Michael gave this young man his first ministry opportunity in a local church. A young man named Martin—as in Martin Luther King Jr.

Michael kept serving those few city blocks, always with a vision for changing them. And they needed change; it was a world of drug dealers, pimps, and gangs, poverty, homelessness, and racism. He knew from the beginning that any real change would rest on leadership. Not just his leadership, but a generation of leaders. Leaders like Martin. But even more to the point, though he never made such a claim, leaders like himself who would take up residence on their own few blocks in areas around the country and around the world where nobody naturally wanted to reside. Blocks that needed truth to set up residence so that it could spread into lives and situations, changing things from the inside out.

So Michael began talking about training leaders, praying about training leaders, casting vision about training leaders, until finally he witnessed its reality. First with a few classes at Twelfth Baptist, then as an extension center of a seminary, and finally as a full-fledged urban campus.

Today you can travel to Roxbury, Massachusetts, and visit the Center for Urban Ministerial Education (CUME) campus. Today, CUME has become one of the leading urban training centers in the United States, teaching each week in six languages, developing hundreds of leaders for urban ministry. Fittingly, it meets in the Michael E. Haynes Academic Building, one block down from Twelfth Baptist, one of Michael's "just three or four city blocks."

Three or four blocks of the *good*.

The Beautiful

Beauty relates to enjoyment and aesthetics, and of the great values, including truth and goodness, it is perhaps the most overlooked. And in a truly decaying culture, it is often the first to lose its moorings.[12] All the more reason to be alarmed by a recent social experiment staged by essayist Gene Weingarten and the *Washington Post*. At 7:51 a.m. on a Friday in the middle of the morning rush hour at the L'Enfant Plaza station of the Washington, DC, Metro, a nondescript, youngish white man in jeans, long-sleeved T-shirt, and Washington Nationals baseball cap removed a violin from a small case. Placing the open case at his feet, he threw in a few dollars to seed the giving and began to play.

But this was no ordinary performer. The fiddler standing against the wall was thirty-nine-year-old Joshua Bell, one of the finest classical musicians in the world, playing some of the most elegant music ever written on a $3.5 million Stradivarius. During the next forty-three minutes, as the violinist performed six classical pieces, 1,097 people passed by.

Did they have time for beauty? Did they even recognize it? No, they did not. Bell was almost entirely ignored. From over a thousand people, only six or seven even took notice.[13]

This goes even deeper than our loss of beauty because of our busy lives. One of the great breaks from the flow of the history of Western thought is our modern tendency to reduce the idea of beauty to a matter of subjective preference as opposed to an objective value. Or even further, a glimpse of the divine. Consider David's great desire to "gaze on the beauty of the LORD" (Ps. 27:4), or the declaration, "From Zion, perfect in beauty, God shines forth" (Ps. 50:2). This was not a subjective assessment—God *is* beauty, and true beauty, wherever it resides, is a glimpse of God himself. And we need more glimpses.

The Power of *Cause*

I've seen the power of *cause* in the hands of our church. People intuitively know the effectiveness of speaking first about our work helping to rescue young girls from the sex-trafficking brothels in the Philippines, and from that to faith in Christ. They lead with telling about our work with local food banks or funding the immediate needs of the working poor, single-parent moms, and the elderly in our city by providing money for bus fare, rent, or heat. It is easy to speak of serving orphans who are among the poorest of the poor in Argentina, building homes for the homeless in Jamaica, or visiting the lonely in a nearby nursing home.

Even if it takes a while to get to talking about Christ, they get there. And they do it with integrity and, most of all, credibility. I've watched the listener soak in Jesus raw and unfiltered along with the scandal of the cross in all of its glorious specificity. Later I've seen those *nones* enfolded into our community and before long, bursting through the waters of baptism. And that's the very best picture of all of the true, the good, and the beautiful.

Questions for Discussion and Reflection

1. Since 2010, *cause* has proven to be the largest area of connection with a lost world, especially when it comes to the *nones*. *Cause* arrests their attention and enlists their participation in the overall community of Christianity. Where have you seen the power of cause recently? How did it affect the lost who participated?

2. What's important to note about the *nones* is that we haven't lost the opportunity to do good *to* them. That means we can show them the love that Jesus sent us to proclaim. That good will open their minds and hearts to the gospel. Are you doing good to those who have no interest in hearing from you? If not, how can you start?

3. The pattern through which the lost are reached has shifted to the following dynamic:

   Nones → Cause → Community → Christ

   This calls for a shift in the evangelistic paradigm. Have you seen the power of this approach to reach the *nones*? What would you have to do to shift your church's approach to meet this new paradigm?

4. Putting *cause* at the forefront of evangelism means many churches will be at a disadvantage due to mundane causes that simply

don't arrest the attention of nonbelievers. What are some causes that you can get involved in that not only will serve the least and the lost but will also stop *nones* in their tracks and force them to pay attention?

5. We must be careful when thrusting ourselves into any cause. The goal is not to right one wrong while creating another. This is tough to discern, but these three things can guide us in our efforts to renew culture: truth, goodness, and beauty. Have you seen someone invest in a cause that did not target truth, goodness, and beauty that then ended poorly?

6. We saw that Old Testament figures like Joseph, Daniel, and Esther worked within the public system in secular settings and were able to affect the system for God. These figures represent a way to renew culture toward the true. Can you think of ways to renew our culture toward the true?

7. Michael Haynes's devotion to his three or four blocks serves as an example of the good. He served an area far from God to bring good where there was much bad. Is there anywhere in your community or in your life where something similar is possible?

8. When a social experiment was staged to have one of the finest classical musicians in the world play in a Washington Metro station, the people missed the genius of the musician because they were too busy to stop and listen. But what was also missed was the beauty of the music itself. How can you and your church introduce beauty to the lost through the causes you champion?

9

Grace and Truth

Missions is often the term used for going overseas for the cause of Christ—hence the word *missionary*. Sadly, it has led some to feel that missions is something that happens "over there," creating a dulled sense of the needs on our doorstep.

When the church is at its best, mission is not something we do; it is something we are. Every day we are on mission to our unchurched friends; every weekend we are on the front lines of bringing Christ to individual lives; every year we expand our influence as we reach out to those who are poor, hungry, or homeless.

The point is that we are missionaries right in our own backyard, but we often don't think to employ basic transcultural missionary practices—only here, we are not crossing between, say, East or West, but between the Christian subculture and the culture of the *nones*.

But if we were to employ basic missiological strategy, what "tasks" would missions entail? Most missiologists would argue that there are three central tasks that are important for any true missionary to do.

The first task for any missionary is to *learn the language* of the people you are trying to reach and then use it. A language barrier is the most elementary and primary obstacle to overcome. Learning the language means educating yourself on how to talk in a way that people can understand and to which they can relate and eventually respond. America has a distinctive and specific language, and it isn't simply English. It is the communication of thoughts and feelings through an understood set of words, sounds, and symbols. It is highly *tribal* and in constant flux.

The second task of a missionary is to *become a student of the culture* and then become so sensitized to that culture that you can operate effectively within it. Culture is the world in which we live and the world that lives in us, which means we are talking about *everything*. Culture is the comprehensive, penetrating context that encompasses our life and thought, art and speech, entertainment and sensibility, values and faith. It serves as the context through which and in which we reach out. While never capitulated to, it must be accommodated.

The third task of the missionary is to *translate the gospel* so that it can be heard, understood, and appropriated. Notice I didn't simply say "translate the Scriptures"—though that is a given. Theologian Millard Erickson, building on the insights of William E. Hordern, offers a helpful distinction in the use of the terms *translation* versus *transformation*. The presentation of the gospel itself must be translated—but never transformed. Every generation must translate the gospel into its own cultural context. This is very different from transforming the message of the gospel into something that was never intended by the biblical witness. Transformation of the message must be avoided at all costs; translation, however, is essential for a winsome and compelling presentation of the gospel of Christ.[1]

So how do we do this? Let's start off with learning the language, and from there move to understanding the culture. I've been doing that for quite a while. Here's a sampling of what a *none* may actually say to you if you are keen to listen:

"I do not consider myself a *pagan*. I mean, really? A pagan? Not sure I like *unchurched* or *irreligious* either, although it's a step up. Ideally, how about John or Mark or Sandra? In other words, my name."

"I honestly don't mind it when you invite me to your church or talk to me about God. Just keep it, I don't know, *natural*. Like when we talk about sports or movies. I hate feeling like a project. Let's keep it a conversation between friends and as friends. I can see doing that."

"Please don't be threatened by my questions. *They really are my questions*, and I've had them for a long time. I hope that if Christianity is true, it can stand up under any amount of intellectual scrutiny. Anyway, I'd feel a lot better if you were less threatened when I raise questions. I'm not trying to be a jerk; I'm just trying to sort it all out, and that means asking you about all kinds of things. I know sometimes it seems combative or aggressive, but God-questions aren't exactly tame—much less safe. And for me, the answers are everything."

"Don't forget that a lot of my junk is emotional, not just intellectual. And it took a lot for me to say that. I almost don't know how to get into this, but I've been burned, disillusioned, and hurt. You may win some of our verbal contests, but it doesn't usually move me forward. It leaves me feeling cold, mostly because some of the time the intellectual stuff is just a smokescreen for what I'm really battling. Here's the last 5 percent: It's not just whether I can buy into this intellectually. It's whether I can buy into it relationally. In other words, are you really *safe*?"

"I would like to *belong* before I *believe*. What I mean is that I'd like to experience this a bit before signing on. Is that legal? I hope so. I think it would be helpful if I could test the waters a bit first."

"There's a lot I don't know, and I know it. Don't make me feel stupid about it—like not knowing much about the Bible or Jesus or whatever. If you could start at the beginning and explain it all to me, that would be great. Like starting with Genesis and moving forward."

"Can we agree that there's a lot of weird stuff attached to Christianity and the Bible? Okay, it may be true, or real, or whatever, but can we just agree that some of it is a bit . . . bizarre? For some strange reason, it would make me feel better to hear you acknowledge how it all looks and sounds to someone from the outside."

"What's up with all the scandals? I'm sympathetic to screwing up, but what makes me want to puke is how they're screwing up while they're telling everybody they don't, or that nobody should, or—you get my point. It just makes the whole thing seem like a joke. Just own that you have screwed up (that'd be fine with me, really; I do it all the time), or just shut up about *not* doing it. But this parading and posturing and then being exposed—it just turns me off. It makes *me* feel like the spiritual one because at least I don't pretend to be something I'm not!"

"I like it when you help people—care for the poor, house the homeless, take care of widows, protect orphans, work for justice against sex-trafficking—that gets my attention and feels authentic. It's also convicting, because I'm not doing much in those areas. I agree with it and write a check now and then, but I'm not on the frontline. When you are, it makes me have to listen to what you say, whether I like it or not."

"I'm really open to it all—more than I let on. In fact, I *want* to feel good about myself spiritually. But I don't think I can ever measure up. When I really think about God, all I feel is guilt and shame, so I stay away. It would be nice if there was something in all of this that made me feel like I could—I don't know—come home?"

Translating the Gospel

With this in mind, as I've listened intently to the growing number of religiously unaffiliated, the dynamics of our message to them has become clear. We must make the dynamic between grace and truth known. Not only is it the heart of the gospel, but it is also at the heart of many of the most regrettable caricatures and stereotypes of Christians.

Three Tasks of a Good Missionary

1. Learn the language: educate yourself on how to talk in a way that people can understand and to which they can relate and eventually respond
2. Study the culture: become so sensitized to that culture that you can operate effectively within it
3. Translate the gospel: translate it into its own cultural context so that it can be heard, understood, and appropriated

---

Unfortunately, many Christians seem confused about how the interplay between grace and truth actually works. For example, it's common to find people and groups separating the two, but it's quite clear that Jesus brought both when he came. In fact, keeping them together is one of the more important exercises for Christian life and thought. As Henry Cloud says, truth without grace is just judgment. Conversely, grace without truth is license.[2]

Let's make a graph with grace on the vertical axis and truth on the horizontal axis (see figure 9.1). Within this, let's draw four quadrants, plotting high and low perspectives of truth in conjunction with high and low views of grace.

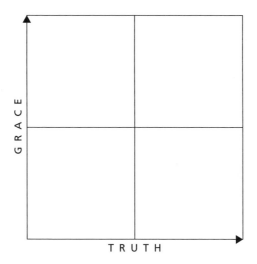

Figure 9.1 Grace and Truth

Each quadrant will represent a way the grace-truth dynamic can be understood, practiced, and then presented to others. Each can also be a paradigm for evaluating entire systems of thought. In fact, a strong case can be made that the various dynamics related to grace and truth form the foundation for what separates Christianity from every other worldview. So getting this one right is essential not only in our message to the *nones* but also our very identity as Christians. So let's begin.

Neither Grace nor Truth

First there is the dynamic of *no grace, no truth*.

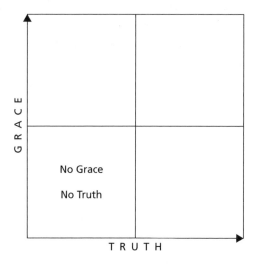

Figure 9.2 No Grace and No Truth

This is reflected in systems of thought and practice based on *karma*, in which there is a cause-effect perspective toward all of life (a lack of grace). It also has a dynamic that makes right and wrong, good and bad either arbitrary or defined by personal choice (the absence of transcendent truth).

Welcome to Hinduism and, in many ways, Buddhism. Both have very little if any sense of binding truth. And in terms of grace, all is determined by karma—the opposite of grace. In Hindu thought, karma is the sum total of your life actions—good and bad. They do not believe that life is linear, going from a beginning to an end. Instead they believe that it is a never-ending circle of life, death, and rebirth. Right now we are reaping the consequences of what we did in an earlier life. If you had good karma in your past life, you are re-incarnated into a good life now. If not, then you will be reincarnated into a life that will not be very pleasant. Your karma even determines what you will be reincarnated as in your next life; you can come back as a human, an animal, or an insect. It's a vicious cycle in which all you get is what you deserve.

You are, no doubt, familiar with the famous story Jesus told of the prodigal son. Here's a twist to the story based on karma. An ancient Asian legend tells the story of another man who had a wayward son:

> The boy became involved with the ruffians of the village who persuaded him to join them in a robbery of his own father's treasury house. After the robbery was over, his friends fled with the stolen treasure and left him to face the guilt of the crime alone. The young man was desperate. He was deserted by his friends, and he had betrayed the trust of his father. But his greatest crime was that he had brought public dishonor on the family name. And, in a culture where ancestors are worshiped and family integrity is a sacred trust, this was the worst wrong of all.
>
> Broken and deeply repentant, he went to his father and begged forgiveness. Graciously, it was granted. The father called all of the members of the family together to celebrate the reconciliation and return of his son. When all had enjoyed the banquet to the fullest, the father stood and lifted his cup of rice wine for a toast. But, as the son drank deeply the contents of his cup, he grabbed his throat and fell lifeless across the table. The son had been poisoned.[3]

But that isn't the Christian message.

I once read an interview in which U2's Bono talked about what draws him to Christianity and has made him even more committed to his Christian faith than ever before. He said, "The one thing that keeps me on my knees is the difference between grace and karma." Then he talked about how every other religion is driven by karma. What you put out comes back to you. An eye for an eye; a tooth for a tooth. Every action met by an equal or opposite reaction.

And then along comes an idea like grace to upend it all. Bono added that grace "is very good news indeed, because I've done a lot of stupid stuff. . . . It doesn't excuse my mistakes, but I'm holding out for grace. I'm holding out that Jesus took my sins onto the cross, because I know who I am, and I hope I don't have to depend on my own religiosity."[4]

Grace without Truth

A second position is high on grace but lacking in truth.

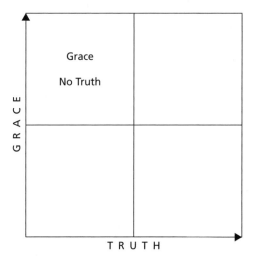

Figure 9.3 Grace but No Truth

If you have grace but no truth, you are left with little more than licentiousness. In other words, almost anything goes in terms of life or thought. This is more than the "cheap grace" that Dietrich Bonhoeffer laments so famously in his classic work, *The Cost of Discipleship*.[5] There, truth existed but it had no teeth; cheap grace dissolves obedience, commitment, and sacrifice. It is received but not responded to. Grace without truth goes further, giving license to virtually any lifestyle and virtually any perspective.

Examples of this position can be found most readily in the Unitarian Universalists, now experiencing rapid growth in the United States. Unitarian Universalists are noted for being accepting of not only everyone but also seemingly everything.[6] I would also argue that this is the unofficial pop culture stance of our day. We are pressed not only to accept people relationally but also to simultaneously affirm whatever decisions or lifestyle choices they make. The joining of acceptance with affirmation is the new definition of acceptance. To not condemn means you must also condone. If you don't condone, you are automatically viewed as condemning.

This flows from confusion over the idea of *tolerance*. When we speak of tolerance, we usually mean *social tolerance*: I accept you as a person. Or at times, *legal tolerance*: you have the right to believe what you wish. We do not, however, tend to mean *intellectual tolerance*. This would mean that all ideas are equally valid. No one believes that ideas supporting genocide, pedophilia, racism, sexism, or rejection of the historical reality of the Holocaust are to be tolerated. But it is precisely the idea of intellectual tolerance that we find our culture sloppily embracing under the overarching mantra of tolerance. And this marks the idea of grace without truth.

Truth without Grace

Then there is truth without grace.

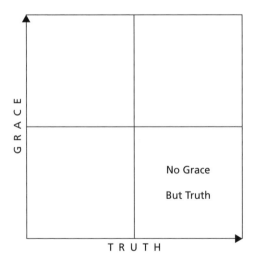

Figure 9.4 No Grace but Truth

This is the worst of legalism and fundamentalism—what many *nones* believe to be the hallmark of the Christian faith. While they may be mistaken in applying this to Christianity (though not always wrong in applying it to certain Christians), they are right in rejecting it for their lives. This is religion at its worst, where there are rules and regulations, dos and don'ts, laws and legalities—but no grace. When there is truth without grace, there is only judgment and condemnation.

The real representative of dogma without grace is Islam. Make no mistake, Muslims believe in truth. The first and most essential doctrine of Islam is that God is one and there is no other God but Allah, and nothing and no one else is to be associated with God. They also hold that God has sent a prophet to every nation to preach the message of there being only one God. These prophets include such biblical characters as Adam, Noah, Abraham, Moses, David, Solomon, Jonah, John the Baptist, and Jesus. Each was sent for a particular age. Muhammad, however, is the last and greatest of the prophets, and the only prophet who is for all time.

Another major Islamic belief is that four of the highest-ranking prophets were given books of divine revelation, or Scriptures. Those four are Moses, who was given the first five books of the Bible; David, who was given the Psalms; Jesus, who was given the Gospels; and Muhammad, who was given the Koran. But only the Koran is considered to have been preserved in an uncorrupted state and exists eternally in Arabic in heaven. So they have their own truth, but not grace.

Another of the five pillars, or beliefs, of Islam is that there is a hierarchy of angels with the angel Gabriel at the top. According to Islam, each person has two angels assigned to him or her—one to record all of that person's good deeds, and the other to record all of his or her bad deeds. Coupled with this is the belief that the God of the Koran has declared that there will be a day when we will all stand before him in judgment. On that day, each person's deeds will be weighed in the balance. Those people whose good deeds outweigh their bad deeds will be rewarded with paradise. Those who have more bad deeds will be sent to hell.

That's quite a difference from the Christian faith. In fact, from 1991 to 2007 Fuller Theological Seminary's School of Intercultural Studies conducted a survey among 750 Muslims who had converted to Christianity. Those surveyed represented fifty ethnic groups from thirty different countries. The reason for becoming Christians? They said that the Koran had produced profound disillusionment because it accentuates God's punishment more than his love, and the use of violence to impose Islamic laws. They said that as Muslims, they could never be certain of their forgiveness and salvation as Christians can. They were attracted to the idea of God's unconditional love.[7]

Grace and Truth

A British conference on comparative religions brought together experts from all over the world to debate what was unique, if anything, about the Christian faith in relation to other religions.

Was it the idea that a god became a man? No, other religions had variations on that one. Even the great Greek myths were about gods appearing in human form.

Was it the resurrection? No. The idea of the dead returning to life could be found in many different ideologies.

Was it heaven, life after death, or an eternal soul?

Was it love for your neighbor, good works, care for the poor and homeless?

Was it about sin or hell or judgment?

The debate went on for some time, until the famous author C. S. Lewis wandered into the room. Lewis himself had journeyed from atheism to agnosticism and then to Christianity. And after that, he became one of the most famous of all Christian writers and thinkers. Lewis asked what the debate was about and found out that his colleagues were discussing what Christianity's unique contribution was among world religions.

"Oh, that's easy," said Lewis. "It's grace." And after they thought about it, they had to agree.

Grace, at its heart, is *getting what you don't deserve and not getting what you do*. The idea of God's love coming to us free of charge, no strings attached, seems to go against every instinct within the human race. The Buddhist eightfold path, the Hindu doctrine of karma, the Jewish covenant, the Muslim code of law—they're all ways to try to earn approval. Only Christianity contends that God's love is unconditional.[8]

Only authentic Christianity brings together both grace and truth. That isn't surprising considering that this is precisely what Jesus

brought when he came. In John's Gospel, a theological bombshell
is offered almost as an offhand comment: "[Jesus] came . . . full of
grace and truth" (John 1:14).

Which brings us to the final quadrant of our grid:

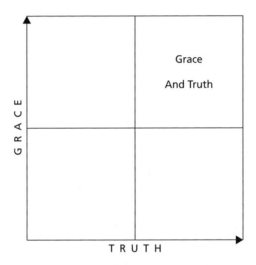

Figure 9.5 Grace and Truth

Jesus accepted the woman at the well in what can only be deemed
by any careful reader in (then) culturally scandalous ways, but he
followed the acceptance by challenging her directly about her serial
promiscuity. He also stopped the stoning of a woman caught in adultery, made it clear he was not going to condemn her, but then pointedly
admonished her to turn from her adulterous ways.

Grace *and* truth flowed from Jesus in a way that can only be deemed
inextricably intertwined. But that's not all. It flowed from him in a
way that was winsome. The very people he challenged about the state
of their lives then wanted him to come to their parties and meet their
friends—and have him challenge them! This is precisely what must
be recaptured if we are to reach this generation of *nones*.

Jesus offered neither a feel-good theology that airbrushed out any
real talk of sin, nor legalistic attitudes of harsh condemnation and

judgment. When he came he brought grace and truth at their best and most compelling.

The Importance of Truth

Let's take the truth dynamic further, because it would be tempting to perceive that the principal problem for Christianity has been offering truth without grace and then going heavy on grace at the expense of truth. Don't.

When you drill deeper into the research surrounding the rise of the *nones*, you will find two interesting dynamics: (1) The negative numbers are coming largely from the falling away of hundreds of thousands of Catholics. Mainline Protestants aren't doing well either. In other words, there's a big loss in the middle of the religious spectrum. (2) The faith groups that *did* see growth were at the *poles*, meaning the far ends of the religious spectrum—the ones with fire in their belly. At one end are the aforementioned *nones*, and on the other are the largely conservative and mostly evangelical nondenominational groups. In other words, the ones who are adamant about believing in nothing in particular or the ones who are adamant about believing in something specific are the only ones attracting converts. The groups on the ends of the spectrum grew to represent about 16 percent each of the population.[9]

It is precisely these *deeper* findings that betray the actual headline regarding the importance of truth accompanying grace. The real headline is that lukewarm religion holds little value in the midst of a settling secularism. What captivates a conscience is anything *gripping*. If a worldview or faith lacks conviction, passion, or life change, then it seems both privately and socially irrelevant.

This means that the only kind of voice that will arrest the attention of the world will be convicting in nature, clear in its message, substantive in its content, and bold in its challenge. It doesn't

> I know your deeds, that you are neither cold nor hot. I wish you were either one or the other! So, because you are lukewarm—neither hot nor cold—I am about to spit you out of my mouth.
>
> Revelation 3:15–16

matter whether it's the brashness of the new atheists like Sam Harris, Christopher Hitchens, or Richard Dawkins, or the unashamed fervor of those embracing Christianity in the Global South. So while those around us may be losing their religion, the good news is that it may remind us to find something we've lost as well: our prophetic voice.

As Mark Galli writes:

> The most needful and difficult task of the church today is to again preach the message of the Cross, and to do so in a way that alarms, surprises, scandalizes, challenges, invigorates, and inspires a 21st-century world. What that would look like exactly is hard to say; our theologians and pastors need to help us here. In the most general terms, it has to be about Christ first and last. It has to be about the Christ who came into the world not to improve generally good people, but to resurrect the dead, not to bolster our self-esteem but to forgive us, not to make people successful but to make them loving, not to win the culture but to establish a kingdom without end. Even more scandalously, the message of the Cross is about a universe saturated with grace, where nothing we have done or can do earns us the right to participate in this stunning new reality; all has been done for us. The best we can do is acknowledge the reality (faith) and begin to live as if it is reality (repent).
>
> The current state of our preaching is driven by an admirable desire to show our age the relevance of the gospel. But our recent attempts have inadvertently turned that gospel into mere good advice—about sex, about social ethics, about how to live successfully. This either offends or bores our culture. A renewed focus on the Cross, articulated in a culturally intelligent way, is the only way forward. Some will be scandalized by it, others will call it foolishness, and yet some will cling to it as salvation. But at least everyone will be talking about that which is truly First and Last.[10]

That is the essence of grace coupled with truth. It is the one message that the world does not seem to be hearing but most desperately needs to hear—and most desperately longs for.

Questions for Discussion and Reflection

1. Read back through the list of what a *none* may say to you. Which of those statements convicted you? Why do you think

that is? And how can you listen to that conviction and channel that energy to effectively evangelize the *nones*?

2. With those statements in mind, what must be made known to the *nones* is the dynamic between grace and truth. Think about your church for a minute. Would a typical attender understand the power of grace and the necessity of truth?

3. Acceptance has a new definition: the joining of acceptance with affirmation. This means that if you don't condone, you also condemn—at least in the minds of the *nones*. How do you move past this confusion of acceptance and affirmation and reach the *nones* with the Good News?

4. Perhaps the worst approach to reaching the lost today is to rank high in truth but low in grace. In other words, people in this category are full of condemnation but have no grace for sinners (like themselves). Consider whether you or your church fall into this category.

5. When we study Jesus's teaching, what we find is that grace and truth are intertwined in ways that are compelling to those he engaged. How can you recapture this dynamic in your teaching and your relationships?

6. Lukewarm religion holds little value in an increasingly secular world. Our causes and convictions must be gripping to the world around us. Are the causes you're engaged in right now gripping to you? Would they be gripping to those outside your church walls?

7. The encouraging thing about grace and truth is that together they hold the message the world so desperately needs to hear—that it even longs to hear. The question is, how do you deliver it in a way that is compelling, convicting, substantive, and bold?

10

A Christian Mind

One of the most overlooked areas related to engaging the culture for Christ, and specifically for engaging the rising numbers of the religiously unaffiliated, is the importance of a Christian mind. This is ironic since it certainly wasn't overlooked by Jesus. When he was confronted by a teacher of the law in Mark 12:28–32, he summarized the great commandment from Deuteronomy 6:4–5: we are to love God with all of our heart, all of our soul, and all of our strength.

But he added, "And with all your mind" (Mark 12:30). It is as if he wanted there to be no doubt that when contemplating the comprehensive nature of a life commitment to God, we should not forget our intellect. But don't reduce that to intellectualism—it's deeper than that.

This is about having a mind developed enough in Christ and for Christ that it is able to contend for Christ in the culture. The biblical vision of the role of the mind is at the heart of the renewal of character and culture. In his manifesto to the Romans, Paul makes this declaration: "Do not conform to the pattern of this world, but be transformed by the renewing of your mind" (Rom. 12:2). The verbs are in the present imperative, which speaks to the challenge to continually *go on* refusing to conform to the patterns of the world and to continually *go on* letting ourselves be renewed by the transforming of our mind. The Phillips paraphrase puts it this way: "Don't let the world around you squeeze you into its own mould" (Rom. 12:2 Phillips). Even better is Eugene Peterson's paraphrase, which reads, "Don't become so well-adjusted to your culture that you fit into it without even thinking" (Rom. 12:2 Message).

Yet Harry Blamires goes so far as to say that "there is no longer a Christian mind . . . a Christian ethic, a Christian practice, a Christian spirituality."[1] As Mark Noll dryly notes, the scandal of the evangelical mind is that there is not much of an evangelical mind.[2] Worse, there is even a bias against the intellect. Richard Hofstadter, in his Pulitzer-prize-winning book, *Anti-Intellectualism in American Life*, identifies "the evangelical spirit" as one of the prime sources of American anti-intellectualism. Hofstadter points out that for many Christians, humble ignorance is a far more noble human quality than a cultivated mind.[3]

> Love the Lord your God with all your heart and with all your soul and with all your mind and with all your strength.
>
> Mark 12:30

Having a Christian mind is thinking in light of God's existence and his self-revelation. Or as Flannery O'Connor referred to herself, it is being a "Christian realist," which reflects her conviction that she lived in the presence of certain theological truths, such as the doctrines of creation, the fall, and redemption. These were not simply matters of subjective belief for her; they were part of the nature of reality, as solid as the laws of physics.[4]

This is at the heart of the challenge. Most of us tend to succumb to a kind of compartmentalization over and against an integrated worldview that addresses the entirety of life. A compartmentalized mind is one that separates the investments of life into distinct categories, such as job, family, HBO, a Bible study, a favorite blog, and a Google search—*all without integration*. Our thinking about one area never informs our thinking about another. So we can be Christians but not reflect about science or technology in light of our faith. Or even worse, never even have the *thought* of reflecting about science or technology in light of our faith come to mind. So issues related to something like bioethics are seldom met with a reasoned reflection on the Scriptures in light of the nature of humanity or the doctrine of creation. It's the same with the worlds of film, literature, economics, politics; many never integrate these areas with thoughtful reflection in light of a Christian worldview.

And *worldview* is a key word. The term itself suggests more than a set of ideas by which you judge other ideas.[5] For example, think of the question, "Where did we come from and who are we?" Only a limited number of answers are at our disposal: we came about by chance (the naturalist contention); we don't really exist (the Hindu response); or we were spoken into existence by God. For the Christian, the answer to that question gives us a foundation for our thinking that no other answer gives. Because we were created, there is value in each person. There is meaning and purpose to every life. There is someone above and outside our existence who stands over it as authority.

Because of this answer, Martin Luther King Jr. could write these words from a Birmingham jail:

> There are two types of law: just and unjust. . . . A just law is a man-made code that squares with the moral law or the law of God. An unjust law is a code that is out of harmony with the moral law. . . . Any law that uplifts human personality is just. Any law that degrades human personality is unjust. All segregation statutes are unjust because segregation distorts the soul and damages the personality.[6]

King's argument was based on the worth of a human being bestowed by God regardless of what other humans may have to say. King laid claim to a law above man's law. No other worldview would have given him the basis for such a claim.

A Battle of Ideas

Make no mistake about the nature of our contest. As John Stott writes, "We may talk of 'conquering' the world for Christ. But what sort of 'conquest' do we mean? Not a victory by force of arms. . . . This is a battle of ideas."[7] This was the concern of Paul when he reminded the Corinthians, "We do not wage war as the world does. . . . We demolish arguments and every pretension that sets itself up against the knowledge of God, and we take captive every thought to make it obedient to Christ" (2 Cor. 10:3, 5). This is the double-edged threat of our day: apart from a Christian mind, either we will be taken captive by the myriad of worldviews contending for our attention or we will fail to make the Christian voice heard above the din. Either way, we begin to think or we lose the fight.

It brings to mind Thomas Cahill's provocatively titled book *How the Irish Saved Civilization*. "Ireland," contends Cahill, "had one moment of unblemished glory. . . . As the Roman Empire fell, as all through Europe matted, unwashed barbarians descended on the Roman cities, looting artifacts and burning books, the Irish, who were just learning to read and write, took up the great labor of copying all of Western literature."[8]

Then missionary-minded Irish monks brought what had been preserved on their isolated island back to the continent, refounding European civilization. And that, Cahill concludes, is how the Irish saved civilization. But there is more at hand in Cahill's study than meets the eye. Beyond the loss of Latin literature and the development of the great national European literatures that an illiterate Europe would not have established, Cahill notes that something else would have perished in the West: "the habits of the mind that encourage thought."[9]

Why does this matter? Cahill continues his assessment, writing that "when Islam began its medieval expansion, it would have encountered scant resistance to its plans—just scattered tribes of animists, ready for a new identity."[10] Without a robust mind to engage the onslaught—and a Christian one at that—the West would have been under the crescent instead of the cross. And while Islam still poses this threat in various places around the world, it is the advance of secularism that looms largest. If we do not form a Christian mind to engage the world, we will have little to offer, and nothing on which to stand. All that to say, never before have the "habits of the mind" mattered more.

The first step in the development of a mind for God is regaining the lost art of thinking itself.[11] Specifically, thinking in relation to how the Christian faith intersects with life and thought.

A New Apologetics

I read recently that the United States Army has instituted a complete overhaul of its basic training regimen—the first such revision in three decades. Largely as a result of what they learned from Iraq and Afghanistan combat veterans, the army is dropping five-mile runs and bayonet drills in favor of zigzag sprints and exercises that hone core muscles. Why? Because soldiers need to be prepared for what really happens in war. And in today's world, the nature of conflict has changed, and it demands a new kind of fitness. Modern combatants must be able to dodge across alleys, walk patrol with heavy packs and body armor, and haul a buddy out of a burning vehicle. Soldiers need to become stronger, more powerful, and more speed driven. They have to know how to roll out of a tumbled Humvee. They have to know how to crawl for their weapons. "They have to understand hand-to-hand combat, to use something other than their weapon, a piece of wood, a knife, anything they can pick up."[12]

It brings to mind how seldom we rethink our own battle strategies, particularly in evangelism—and perhaps most of all in the field of apologetics. If used at all, more often than not we cling to Enlightenment-era approaches that attempt to answer Enlightenment-era questions. This is all well and good, and the challenges of the Enlightenment are not as absent from our cultural landscape as many may think. After all, anyone who has even the most rudimentary knowledge of intellectual history knows such questions didn't originate with the Enlightenment. And even more to the point, anyone who actually dialogues with those who are exploring Christianity knows that they remain alive and well, particularly in the early stages of investigation. Just remind yourself of the popularity of the writings of Christopher Hitchens, Bart Ehrman, and Richard Dawkins, the novels of Dan Brown, and the media assaults of Bill Maher.

But I am far from alone in noting that the questions *nones* are asking of Christianity, if they bother to ask at all, have changed significantly in recent years. For example, I do not encounter very many people who ask questions that classical apologetics trained us to answer, such as questions related to the existence of God. Instead, the new questions have to do with significance and meaning.

One common question is, "So what?" As in, "So what if Jesus rose from the dead?" You thought you were done once you demonstrated that there was an empty grave and that no other explanation—save a resurrection—could account for the absence of a body. You thought the goal was winning a logical, empirically driven argument.

Think again. People need common intellectual barriers removed, but it quickly progresses to the heart of the matter: *meaning*. They have seen few, if any, lives that have truly had their deepest needs intersected by Christ. They do not know the difference a life in relationship with Christ really makes.

There are also a great many questions about the character of God. "What kind of God is the God of the Bible?" It is not uncommon to find direct challenges such as, "Is this God of yours really that good? Is he really that moral?" I recently read of an outreach pastor who has come to similar conclusions: "The questions [people are asking] have changed quite significantly in the past thirty years. It used to be, 'Is there a God?' and now it's 'What I know about God I don't like.' Their biggest complaint is that God acts in morally inferior ways compared to us."[13]

Granted, pointed questions are not new. This is not the first generation to claim that God is a bully, sounds vengeful and angry and over-anxious to consign people to hell, or seems a bit too worked up over sexual ethics. This is far from the first era of human history during which people have wondered aloud why God becoming a human and dying for our sins was necessary, much less why he allows human suffering to go on. What *is* new is the kind of questions being asked and the importance of answering these questions with an openness and transparency that acknowledge the worth of the question. Like never before, we are being called to defend and explain God's character, clear up misunderstandings of who the God of the Bible actually is, and explain the Christian faith in ways that people in a post-Christian world now need it explained. If we don't, we will lose people. And some of those people will grow up and influence a lot of other people to get lost along with them.

Consider Dan Brown, author of *The Da Vinci Code*. In an interview to promote a new book, he was asked, "Are you religious?" Here is his answer:

I was raised Episcopalian, and I was very religious as a kid. Then, in eighth or ninth grade, I studied astronomy, cosmology, and the origins of the universe. I remember saying to a minister, "I don't get it. I read a book that said there was an explosion known as the Big Bang, but here it says God created heaven and earth and the animals in seven days. Which is right?" Unfortunately, the response I got was, "Nice boys don't ask that question." A light went off, and I said, "The Bible doesn't make sense. Science makes much more sense to me." And I just gravitated away from religion.[14]

This was a question that should have been *immediately* affirmed as worthwhile and then quickly sorted out in relation to the biblical materials. It simply wasn't that difficult to sort out. God could have certainly used the Big Bang to create the universe. The Bible tells us *that* God did it, not *how*. But it wasn't answered. So a young boy went looking for a better God. One who would be open to questions, and hopefully, would offer some answers. What's tragic is that he actually had that God. But nobody told him.

Mere Christians

One intriguing idea is that the entire *rise of the nones* will prove to be the seedbed for renewal. Krista Tippett, the Yale Divinity School grad who hosts *On Being* on public radio, is one such proponent. When asked about the *nones* in an interview, she answered, "On the 'nones,' I actually take a little bit of a radical view: That some of them may be a crucible of renewing and reforming religion in the coming period." After noting the small number that are actually atheists, she added:

> I think a lot these days about Dietrich Bonhoeffer in Germany in the mid-twentieth century. . . . He had seen the [church] cease to be the carrier of its own heart and soul and its virtues and its theology. . . . He started thinking about this notion of a religionless Christianity. His idea was that Christianity brings truths into the world that will survive and be resurrected even as the institutions and the structures and the words fail.

I don't know this for sure, but I do believe there is something in that [*nones*] movement that, fifty or one hundred years from now, we may look back and say that was a crucible in renewal.[15]

I actually find this an intriguing idea, but one that is contingent on authentic Christian faith actually being preserved during the rejection by the institutional alliance. It would be akin to the "mere Christianity" argued for by C. S. Lewis. The dilemma is that a robust orthodoxy, rising above and beyond institutional religion, is not being preserved as part of the spirituality of the *nones*. It's not even preserved within those who profess to hold to the Christian faith. Consider the U.K., where the rise of the *nones* has a few years' head start on our own escalation. A 2012 survey by the Theos think tank found that only 31 percent of all professing Christians in the U.K. believe Jesus rose from the dead; 41 percent believe in life after death. One out of every four prefer the very un-Christian idea of reincarnation.[16]

The passion of C. S. Lewis was thoughtfully translating the Christian faith into language that everyone can understand. He was driven to have people know what Christianity is *about*. It was through a series of radio addresses given over the BBC during World War II that the evidence of his intellectual labors—along with his conversational style, wit, intellect, and rough charm—first revealed Christianity to millions. The initial invitation was for four fifteen-minute talks. The response was so overwhelming that they gave him a fifth segment to answer listeners' questions.

Then a second round of talks was requested and given. The clarity of thought, along with his ability to gather together a wide range of information and make it plain, led one listener to remark that they "were magnificent, unforgettable. Nobody, before or since, has made such an 'impact' in straight talks of this kind."[17] The BBC asked for a third round of talks, this time stretching out for eight consecutive weeks. Lewis consented, but made it clear it would be his last. His goal throughout his writings was simple. It was "to expound 'mere' Christianity, which is what it is and was what it was long before I was born."[18]

His talks were eventually gathered together in a single work titled *Mere Christianity*, and the book continues to make Christianity known to millions. You may have heard of this book. Its appeal rests on two levels. The first is as a first-rate work of apologetics, meaning a case for the Christian faith. But on a second level, it is because of the dynamic inherent within the title. The twentieth century's most accomplished apologist for the Christian faith had little desire to stake out narrow theological ground. He wanted to map out a vast territory on which individuals could gather. Rather than being less intellectual, in many ways it was more. It was scholarship, not academics, and scholarship is always more winsome and compelling.

If you are like me, you probably desire "mere Christianity." It is a phrase first coined by the seventeenth-century Anglican writer Richard Baxter. Baxter lived through the English Civil War and, as a Puritan, threw his support behind Oliver Cromwell and the Parliamentary forces. It was Cromwell who summoned Baxter from his church in Kidderminster, Worcestershire, to help establish the *fundamentals of religion* for the new government. Baxter complied, but Cromwell complained that Baxter's summary of Christianity could be affirmed by a Papist. "So much the better," replied Baxter.

As Alan Jacobs writes in his exceptional biography of Lewis, Baxter's challenge was his refusal to allow Christianity to succumb to the spirit of fashion and sect. He was convinced that there was a core of orthodox Christianity that Puritans, Anglicans, and Catholics all affirmed and that should have been a source of peace among them.

> "Must you know what Sect or Party I am of?" he wrote in 1680. "I am against all Sects and dividing Parties: but if any will call Mere Christian by the name of a Party, . . . I am of that Party which is so against Parties. . . . I am a CHRISTIAN, a MERE CHRISTIAN, of no other religion."
> . . . If the danger in Baxter's time had been warfare among various kinds of Christians, the danger in Lewis's time was the evaporation of Christianity altogether. Yet Lewis felt that the remedy for the first crisis was also the remedy for the second: if Christianity is embattled and declining, it is all the more important for Christians to put their differences aside and join to sing the One Hymn of the One Church.[19]

Mere Christianity is not a reduction of orthodoxy—truth on the lowest level, as it were—but the distillation of Christianity so that it is fermented to its fullest potency. It is the essence of Christianity, stripped of all matters unrelated to its pulsating energy.

Statue of Richard Baxter at St. Mary's Kidderminster, Worcestershire, England

In a day marked by the rising of the *nones*—those who claim no religious affiliation and, in fact, detest any and all labels—it is perhaps time to renew ourselves to what Baxter and Lewis championed. Because a *mere* Christian may be the only kind that can get through to a *none* world.

Questions for Discussion and Reflection

1. It's worth nothing that when Jesus quotes Deuteronomy in the book of Mark, he adds to the summary of all the commandments

to love God "with all your mind" (Mark 12:30). Why do you think Jesus adds this?

2. John Stott says, "We may talk of 'conquering' the world for Christ. But what sort of 'conquest' do we mean? Not a victory by force of arms. . . . This is a battle of ideas."[20] Do you view conquering the world for Christ in this way? How would it change your approach if you did?

3. The habits of the mind are as important now as they have ever been with the looming rise in secularism. What habits have you formed to further shape a mind for God?

4. Increasingly a different kind of question is being asked about faith. Apologetics hasn't traditionally been prepared to answer this question, which is, "So what?" "So what if Jesus rose from the dead?" "So what if I'm a sinner?" What are some ways you can answer these questions and prepare your mind to engage this kind of debate?

5. Mere Christianity, the kind espoused by C. S. Lewis so famously, may be the only kind of Christianity that can get through to a *none* world. Mere Christianity is the distillation of Christianity, not a reduction of orthodoxy. As such, it's time for a renewed interest in mere Christianity. How can you apply the principles of Lewis's (and Baxter's) approach to mere Christianity in your life and in your church?

6. The best way to sum up this chapter and to clearly understand the importance of having a Christian mind is to reread and reflect on these words from earlier in the chapter: "Like never before, we are being called to defend and explain God's character, clear up misunderstandings of who the God of the Bible actually is, and explain the Christian faith in ways that a post-Christian world now needs it explained. If we don't, we will lose people."

11

The Importance of Unity

The CNN program *Crossfire*, which boasted being about left versus right, black versus white, paper versus plastic, the Red Sox against the Yankees, had daringly invited comedian Jon Stewart on to the show after Stewart criticized them for their acerbic banter. Each week, two guests espousing opposing views were brought on to duke it out, and Stewart had denigrated the bloodshed. Although they were hoping, no doubt, for more sparks to fly, Stewart disarmed the hosts with words they did not expect: "Why do we have to fight?"[1]

It was a good question. So good that shortly thereafter the show was canceled due to declining ratings, not altogether separate from repeated airings of Stewart's appearance on YouTube. (However, CNN has recently revived the program with new hosts.)

So why *do* we have to fight?

Sociologist Deborah Tannen writes that we live in an "argument culture." Her observation is that we no longer dialogue with each other, contending that there has been a system-wide relational breakdown in our culture. It is as if we approach everything with a warlike mentality, so we end up looking at the world—and people—in an adversarial frame of mind.

How do we explore an idea?

A debate.

How do we cover the news?

Find people who express the most extreme, polarizing views and present them as the two sides.

How do we settle a dispute?

Through litigation that pits one party against the other.

How do we begin an essay?

Oppose someone—for criticizing and attacking shows that you are really thinking.[2]

The lack of civility in our world has become so pandemic that it is now widely chronicled as a cultural phenomenon. Consider a *USA Today* article titled, "Rudeness, Threats Make the Web a Cruel World," or a *New York Times* article on the impolite side of Wikipedia.[3] Peter Wood, in his book *A Bee in the Mouth*, speaks of this in terms of "anger in America."[4] Sadly, it is this anger that seems to mark the very people who should be most immune to such animus: *Christians.*

This was illustrated in what has been voted the best "religious" joke of all time. Comedian Emo Philips tells of walking across a bridge and seeing a man standing on the edge, ready to jump off. He ran over and said, "Stop! Don't do it!"

"Why shouldn't I?" the man said.

"Well, there's so much to live for."

"Like what?"

"Well, are you religious?"

The man said, "Yes."

I said, "Me too! Are you Christian or Buddhist?"

"Christian."

"Me too! Are you Catholic or Protestant?"

"Protestant."

"Me too! Are you Episcopalian or Baptist?"

"Baptist."

"Wow, me too! Are you Baptist Church of God or Baptist Church of the Lord?"

"Baptist Church of God!"

"Me too! Are you original Baptist Church of God or Reformed Baptist Church of God?"

"Reformed Baptist Church of God!"

"Me too! Are you Reformed Baptist Church of God, reformation of 1879, or Reformed Baptist Church of God, reformation of 1915?"

His new friend replied, "Reformed Baptist Church of God, reformation of 1915."

To which Philips replied, "Die, heretic!" and he pushed him off.[5]

I've Got Enough Problems in My Life

A recent editorial in *Christianity Today* discusses how no attribute of civilized life seems more under attack than civility.[6] The author, David Aikman, notes the extent to which certain Christians have turned themselves into

> the self-appointed attack dogs of Christendom. They seem determined to savage not only opponents of Christianity, but also fellow believers of whose doctrinal positions they disapprove. A troll through the Internet reveals websites so drenched in sarcasm and animosity that an agnostic, or a follower of another faith tradition interested in what it means to become a Christian, might be permanently disillusioned.[7]

I once read of a large church that made the news due to a problem with a persistently caustic blogger. A former member, he had become disgruntled over various actions of the senior pastor, and he became further incensed that said pastor maintained the backing of the leadership. With nowhere to go with his frustration and no means to lobby for his cause, he started an anonymous blog to wage a one-person campaign of accusation and bitterness. It quickly disintegrated on both sides to such a degree that suits and countersuits began flying freely. What a godforsaken mess.

The article I was reading about this had links that led to other links, and before I knew it, I found myself exposed in a way I had never imagined possible to the sordid world of the bitter blog—blogs that seemingly exist for no other reason than to attack a particular Christian leader, church, ministry, or movement. More often than not, the divides were over nothing more than a disagreement about negligible points of theology, varying philosophies of ministry, or differing styles of leadership.

As mentioned in an earlier chapter, when I started Mecklenburg Community Church in the early 1990s, I commissioned a survey through the Barna Research Group to ask unchurched people who lived in the surrounding community a simple but direct question: "Why don't you go to church?" The leading answers fell into categories you may expect:

"There is no value in attending."

"I don't have the time."

"I'm simply not interested."

"Churches ask for money too much."

"Church services are usually boring."

What surprised me most was the strength of one response in particular—so strong it was the second most common answer for being unchurched, representing six out of every ten people:

"Churches have too many problems."[8]

The assessment of the unchurched continues to follow suit: the typical Christian community is inflexible, hypocritical, judgmental, and just plain mean. Division and discord are perceived to be more present in church than in many other groups. Why would anyone want to become involved with something that, in his or her mind, is so obviously dysfunctional? As one man in the survey quipped, "I've got enough problems in my life. Why would I go to church and get more?"

Sadly, this is not new for American Christianity. I once read of a school president, who was also an evangelist, who made it clear that if any faculty or student attended a certain fellow evangelist's crusade, they would be fired or expelled. If they wanted to pray for the evangelist, he suggested the following words:

Dear Lord, bless the man who leads Christian people into disobeying the word of God, who prepares the way for Antichrist by building the apostate church and turning his so-called converts over to infidels and unbelieving preachers. Bless the man who

*flatters the Pope and defers to the purple and scarlet-clothed
Antichrist who heads the church that the word of God describes
as the old whore of Babylon.*[9]

So much for Bob Jones Sr. of Bob Jones University and his relationship with the famed evangelist Billy Graham. I am sure Bob Jones Sr.
was a good and godly man in many ways. Just not in this way. While
sentiments of this kind have been brewing for some time, what's
new is the increasingly public nature of our vitriol, its widespread
dissemination through the internet, and our growing comfort and
even affirmation of its manifestation. As Francis Schaeffer observed
toward the end of his life, it has almost become a matter of personal
privilege: "We rush in, being very, very pleased, it would seem at times,
to find other men's mistakes. We build ourselves up by tearing other
men down . . . we love the smell of blood, the smell of the arena, the
smell of the bullfight."[10]

We may be pleased, but we are not being Christian—not to mention appealing, especially to the *nones*.

The Mark of a Christian

While we have already explained the importance of *cause* eclipsing
community for arresting the attention of the *nones*, that does not
relegate *community* to the backwaters of concern. While it may not
be as important for attraction, it is paramount for affirmation.[11]

In the Gospel of John we have the poignant final words and prayers
of Jesus regarding his present and future disciples before he went to
the cross. Between John 13 and John 17, Jesus poured out his heart.
It is considered by many to be among the most moving sections of
the New Testament.

What occupied Jesus the moments before his atoning for the sins of
the world? Not surprisingly, he was concerned that the world would
recognize his gift. And how would that happen? Christ's torrent of
prayer and pleading begins and ends with a passionate call for unity
among those who did and would claim his name. The observable
love between those who called themselves his followers was seen by

> My prayer is not for them alone. I pray also for those who will believe in me through their message, that all of them may be one, Father, just as you are in me and I am in you. May they also be in us so that the world may believe that you have sent me. I have given them the glory that you gave me, that they may be one as we are one—I in them and you in me—so that they may be brought to complete unity. Then the world will know that you sent me and have loved them even as you have loved me. Father, I want those you have given me to be with me where I am, and to see my glory, the glory you have given me because you loved me before the creation of the world.
>
> John 17:20–24

Jesus to be *everything*. Why? Jesus said it would be this unity, and this unity alone, that would arrest the world's attention in such a way as to confirm that he is from the Father.

We often marvel at the growth of the early church, the explosion of faith in Christ in such numbers and speed that in only a blink of history the Roman Empire had officially turned from paganism to Christianity. We look for formulas and programs, services and processes, strategies and techniques. The simpler truth is that first they shared the gospel like it was gossip over the backyard fence.[12] But what did they subsequently observe in the communal life of the messenger who shared that gossip? As Tertullian notes, the awed pagan reaction to the Christian communal life was, "See how they love one another."[13]

As is often pointed out, when the Bible speaks about such loving unity, it doesn't mean uniformity, which is everyone looking and thinking alike. The biblical idea of unity is also not to be confused with unanimity, which is complete agreement about every petty issue across the board—though within individual churches there should be unity of purpose and an agreement on the major issues related to doctrine and mission. By *unity* the Bible means first and foremost a oneness of heart—a *relational* unity. Being kind to one another, gracious to one another, forgiving of one another. It is not about assuming the worst, shooting the wounded, or being quick to be suspicious. Biblical unity is about working through conflicts, avoiding slander and gossip, and being generous in spirit. It is giving each other the benefit of the

Defining the "U" Words

Unity ≠ Uniformity

Uniformity means everyone looking and thinking alike.

Unity ≠ Unanimity

Unanimity means complete agreement about every petty issue across the board as it relates to the church.

Unity = Relational Unity

Relational unity means being kind to one another, gracious to one another, forgiving of one another—not assuming the worst, shooting the wounded, or being quick to be suspicious.

doubt, distributing ample doses of grace in the midst of our sin and imperfection, and demonstrating fierce loyalty.

Such unity matters—so much so that the Bible reserves some of its harshest words of discipline for those who sin against it. "Warn a divisive person once, and then warn them a second time. After that, have nothing to do with them," writes the apostle Paul to Titus (Titus 3:10). And in one of the most overlooked passages of Scripture, Paul warns strongly against taking the Lord's Supper—the sacrament portraying our vertical unity with Christ and then the horizontal unity with others that resulted from it—if you have unresolved relational conflict in your life. So strongly was God's feeling on this that Scripture tells us that it could result—and indeed had resulted—in the death of those who so violated the sacrament.

This shouldn't surprise us. As we take of the body of Christ, we are to *be* the body of Christ. Paul writes:

> Is not the cup of thanksgiving for which we give thanks a participation in the blood of Christ? And is not the bread that we break a participation in the body of Christ? Because there is one loaf, we, who are many, are one body, for we all share the one loaf. (1 Cor. 10:16–17)

The symbolic act of sharing from one loaf symbolizes the unity of the body of Christ, the church, which has as its source of nourishment the bread of life. The very word *companion* is from two Latin words, *com*, which means "with," and *panis*, which means "bread." So the word *companion* literally means "with bread" or "breadfellow." We are companions because we are together through the bread, which is the body of Christ. From this comes Paul's charge:

> In the following directives I have no praise for you, for your meetings do more harm than good. In the first place, I hear that when you come together as a church, there are divisions among you. . . . When you come together [in this way] it is not the Lord's Supper you eat. (1 Cor. 11:17–20)

As Francis Schaeffer points out, such love is *the* mark of the Christian. Not just a feeling of love or an acknowledgment of love, but a *demonstration* of love. And it is not simply decisive to our faith, but also to our witness. As Schaeffer observes, drawing from the biblical witness:

> Jesus is giving a right to the world. Upon his authority he gives the world the right to judge whether you and I are born-again Christians on the basis of our observable love toward all Christians.
>
> That's pretty frightening. Jesus turns to the world and says, "I've something to say to you. On the basis of my authority, I give you a right: you may judge whether or not an individual is a Christian on the basis of the love he shows to all Christians."[14]

It should be deeply convicting that the secular marketplace understands the importance of this more than many Christians do. It is understood that people expect great performance from products, services, and experiences. So what makes some brands inspiring while others languish? Saatchi and Saatchi, a leading marketing firm, coined the term *Lovemarks* to reveal the answer, calling it the "future beyond brands."

When applied to business, the four quadrants in figure 11.1 are easily grasped and applied. Something in the lower left quadrant—the low love, low respect category—has little loyalty. It may be necessary, but it's just a commodity. Think about the US airline industry. Something in the lower right quadrant—the high love, low respect area—is little more than a fad. Think Snooki and *Jersey Shore*.

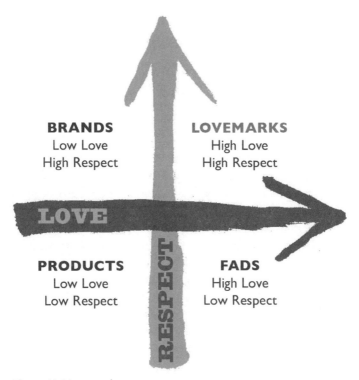

Figure 11.1 Lovemarks

If you move into the upper left quadrant—the low love, high respect area—you have your typical brand. You may respect that brand, but if something better comes along, you won't think twice about switching. Think Proctor and Gamble or General Electric.

But then you have the Holy Grail of branding. In the upper right area, you have both high love and high respect. Kevin Roberts, author of *Lovemarks: The Future Beyond Brands*, does not call this a product, a fad, or a brand; he calls it a Lovemark.[15] Lovemarks deliver beyond expectations, sitting at the top of high levels of respect. They reach our hearts as well as our minds, creating an intimate, emotional connection that we don't want to live without. Take a brand away and people will find a replacement. Take a Lovemark away and people will protest its absence. You don't just buy Lovemarks, you embrace them passionately—you experience them.[16] In the business world, think Apple when you think of Lovemarks. In American politics, think John F. Kennedy or Ronald Reagan.

Christianity is meant to be the ultimate Lovemark, and in light of our mission to the world, it must be. Schaeffer is right when he maintains that the world cares little for doctrine. One thing and one thing only, Schaeffer asserts, will confirm the truth of a message to a world that has disavowed the very idea of truth: "The love that true Christians show for each other and not just for their own party." This is, Schaeffer concludes, the final apologetic. Unloving attitudes and words cause a "stench that the world can smell. . . . Our sharp tongues, the lack of love between us . . . these are what properly trouble the world."[17]

The dilemma is that it does not always seem to trouble us, and usually for two reasons: The first is that we simply do not see it as sin. It has become so commonplace, we no longer feel conviction. I recall talking to the president of a leading Christian seminary. He said that soon after his appointment, when he went to his first faculty meeting as president, he couldn't believe the way the professors were talking to each other and the spirits that were being portrayed. The dialogue was negative, nasty, biting, vitriolic, and unloving. Afterward, sensing he was shocked at the interplay, someone said to him, "Don't worry—that was normal—it's just the way we talk around here."

He couldn't help himself. "Well," he said, "it sure sounded like sin to me!" And he was right. It *was* sin.

The second reason it does not trouble us is this: It is not simply the *acceptance* of lovelessness that leads to its continued presence but our *justification* of it. Specifically, the warped theology that is often embraced says loving actions and attitudes are only warranted when you have nothing provoking you otherwise. It is as if disagreement, disapproval, and disenchantment sanction bad behavior. The *bitter blog* is justified *because*; the slanderous attack is warranted *because*; the angry accusation can be made *because*. A pastor friend of mine, drawn to it time and again, compared it to the lure of pornography.

And make no mistake. Like pornography, it doesn't just sound like sin, or look like sin, or feel like sin. It *is* sin. And it is keeping the message of Christ from being confirmed in the hearts and the minds of those we are charged to reach.

Questions for Discussion and Reflection

1. We often find ourselves viewing the world and our culture with an adversarial frame of mind. Well-intentioned debates become caustic, blogs become bitter, and the cause we trumpet ends up being drowned out by our rhetoric. Think carefully about your approach to debate and discourse. Do you fall into the trap of the adversarial mindset? If so, how can you combat that tendency?

2. This adversarial frame of mind has crept into the very people who should be most immune to it—Christians. Have you seen this creeping effect in your own church, or perhaps another church around you?

3. A common perception of *nones* and other unchurched people is that the church is full of problems. Do you take that point of view seriously and take care to make sure you don't prove their point?

4. Community is a powerful force for affirming the *nones* when they come through your doors. Not affirmation of their lifestyle, but of their standing as sinners and people in need of a Savior. Does your community welcome those outside the church? Would a *none* feel loved, accepted, and dignified by those in your community?

5. Just before his death on the cross, Jesus made a passionate plea for unity among believers because this alone has the power to arrest the attention of the world and confirm that Jesus was in fact God in human form. Is that plea for unity playing out in your church? Do you actively try to cultivate an environment of love and unity?

6. If your church does take this call to unity seriously, you should witness things like working through conflicts, avoiding gossip, and giving the benefit of the doubt. This is primarily what the Bible means by *unity*. It's a relational unity that weaves between and inside a group of believers. Does that kind of unity emanate from your community?

7. Francis Schaeffer notes that Jesus gave a harrowing right to the world: "Upon his [Jesus's] authority he gives the world the

right to judge whether you and I are born-again Christians on the basis of our observable love toward all Christians."[18] If ten unchurched people show up at your church this weekend, what will their consensus be based on the love (or lack of love) they witness?

8. One of the most dangerous deceptions in the church today is that unloving attitudes are not sin. They have become so commonplace that instead of being recognized as the sin they are, they're written off as "the way things are done." Do you honestly see unloving attitudes as sin, or do you write them off as part of the process?

9. Another reason unloving attitudes seem to no longer trouble us is that the continued acceptance of that spirit leads to its continued justification. When an unloving spirit is tolerated, it's considered to be justified. Not to say that is correct thinking, but that's how it works nonetheless. Are you accepting of unloving attitudes in your staff, congregation, or teams? What can you do to address this immediately and move toward the unity Jesus pleaded with us to have?

12

Opening the Front Door

When Bill Clinton ran for the presidency in 1992, eventually scoring an upset victory over incumbent George H. W. Bush, his political strategist James Carville made it very clear what their overarching strategy would be. Hanging in every office was a singular sign for all to see: "It's the economy, stupid!"

And that really was the issue of the election. It determined who won and who lost. Thanks to Carville, Clinton focused relentlessly on that issue.

Bush didn't. Clinton won.

I once made a sign for our staff that you can still see hanging on cubicles and office walls around Meck. It too is simple. It reads: "It's the weekend, stupid!" And in many ways, it is.

I almost didn't include this chapter, but the more I thought about it, the more I was convinced it was worth the risk. The risk is that it will be dismissed as passé in terms of outreach strategy or relevance to reaching the *nones*.[1]

During the 1980s and '90s there was an approach to outreach that could be caricatured as "the big show," as in large, highly produced, glitzy services that were presentational in nature. There was professional music, clever drama sketches, and Disneyesque light displays.

A reaction of sorts set in during the 2000s that shifted toward a more stripped-down, communal, "authentic" approach that was often labeled "missional," meaning moving from "come and see" to "let's go and be."

But this is where it matters that a practitioner is writing this instead of an academic. Those who discounted the presentational approach threw out the baby with the bathwater. Quick—name one church that stripped everything down, went totally with a "let's go and be" approach (as opposed to having a service or event that allowed individuals to invite their friends) that experienced breakout growth among the *nones*.

Exactly.

Many got some serious press for being uber-hip, but not much happened in terms of numbers. The truth is that there is a need to be *incarnational* in the world as individual followers of Christ. There is also enormous power in pulling together our resources and gifts as a community of faith for intentional outreach where singers sing, communicators communicate, those gifted with children work with the young, and so on. In other words, it is strategic for the individual witness of believers to join forces with the collective work of the church to penetrate our culture for Christ. It's true in terms of *cause*, meaning pulling together for large-scale efforts that arrest the attention of the world, but it's also true in terms of the actual activity of evangelism.

Am I arguing for a return to the old "seeker service" strategy? Yes and no. No in regard to its 1980s form, but yes in terms of how it has manifest itself for over two thousand years. Don't forget: it wasn't invented in South Barrington, Illinois, in 1975. Jesus had an individual *and* a crowd-based approach to evangelism. So did the apostles. So did the early church. So did the Reformers. So did individuals such as Charles Wesley, D. L. Moody, and Billy Graham.

If the church has a "front door," and it clearly does, why shouldn't it be opened wide and then strategically developed for optimal impact for any and all *nones* who may venture inside? I already hear you: "But isn't that your point? They aren't going to venture inside? So why bother?" That is why I'm including this chapter. They *will* venture inside, just not on their own. There's one thing that 82 percent of all unchurched people can't seem to resist. It cuts through their

defenses and penetrates their barriers. According to surveys at LifeWay
Research, 82 percent of them seem to
have a single weakness: *if a friend,
or someone they know, invites them
to church.* Reread that: 82 percent of
all unchurched people would come
to church this weekend if they were

> **Fast Fact**
>
> Of all unchurched people, 82 percent would come to church this weekend if they were invited by a friend.
>
> LifeWay Research

invited by a friend.[2] And if you could get them there, imagine what
you could achieve. They could be exposed to the collective energies,
gifts, resources, and influence of your church at its best.

But how should your church be positioned, optimally, for the *nones?*
How do you open the front door to someone you have invited who
may actually come? We've talked about the message conveying grace
and truth, but there is so much more, beginning with something as
simple as friendliness.

Friendliness

In an interesting study, the Technical Assistance Research Program study
for the White House Office of Consumer Affairs found that 96 percent
of unhappy customers never complain about rude or unfriendly treatment, but 90 percent of those unhappy customers will not return to
the place where that unfriendliness was manifest. Further, each one
of those unhappy customers will tell nine other people about the lack
of friendliness and courteousness, and 13 percent will tell more than
twenty other people.[3] A later study by the same organization discovered
that the number one reason individuals do not return to a particular
establishment is an indifferent, unfriendly employee's attitude.[4]

Now, we all know that every church thinks it's friendly. I've never
met a church yet where the people said, "Yeah, we're mean and proud
of it!" No! Every church *thinks* it's friendly. But what that means is:

they are friendly to each other

they are friendly to people they know

they are friendly to people they like

they are friendly to people who are like them

That's not friendliness; that's a clique or, at best, a club.

To prove the point, another recent LifeWay Research survey found that while three out of every four churchgoers say they have significant relationships with people at their church, they admit they don't make an effort with new people. In fact, only one in every six even try.[5] That's not very friendly.

This needs to be a cultivated part of your DNA. At Meck, we've worked very hard to be intentional about something that many may feel can only be left to chance. We've built an entire ministry around it called Guest Services, and it oversees greeters, ushers, hospitality, and much more—all geared toward the experience of first impressions and friendliness. It's one of our largest and most strategic efforts.

But friendliness holds more than a smile and a welcome. It has to do with an atmosphere of acceptance. Two words are key here: *atmosphere* and *acceptance*.

First, *atmosphere*. Churches have cultures—a DNA if you will. The goal is to cultivate one that is accepting. If you are going to reach the *nones*, they are going to come to you *as a none*. That means they will come as couples living together, as gay couples, pregnant outside of marriage, addicted, skeptical. Is that going to raise an eyebrow? Or is it taken in stride in a way that makes the person feel instantly at ease? At Meck, it's just another day of normal.

Then there is the *acceptance* itself. Acceptance is not affirmation, but it *is* an embrace. It involves starting where people actually are, warts and all, and then loving them, caring for them, and enveloping them into the community. This is more key than you may think. It is one thing to create a welcoming atmosphere; it is another to actually wrap your arms around someone who is sin-stained and sin-soaked in an effort to lead him or her to the cross. In other words, it's ministry in the trenches. It means talking about marriage to those who are living together; it means helping teenagers involved in cutting or hooking up; it means working with a Christian wife who has a non-Christian husband who wants them to enter an "open" marriage; it means going as pastors to a house that seems to be demonically influenced because of the occupants' past occult activity; and so much more.

All to say, an atmosphere of acceptance is also a culture of involvement and investment in the trenches of lives that have been lived and ordered apart from Christ. It's time to get a church life of little more than potluck dinners out of your head.

Children's Ministry

When our kids were young, my family and I went to a church while on our summer study break; it was a new church, very small, that was meeting in a movie theater. How can I say this? It was one of the most programming-challenged services I've ever attended. It was so bad that we were looking at our watches *five minutes* after the service started. When the service mercifully ended, we wanted to get out of there and never return. I know, that isn't very gracious, and I should have been focused more on worshiping Jesus—but you would have wanted to leave too.

But when we went to pick up our kids, they were having an absolute blast. They didn't want to leave! There was a couple who poured themselves into that ministry and made it really, really good. I still recall how

---

Keys to Having an Open Front Door

- *Friendliness*—You must be intentional about the guest's experience and cultivate an atmosphere of acceptance.
- *Children's Ministry*—Children are the heart of your growth engine. And if *nones* ever come to your church uninvited, it will probably be for the sake of their kids.
- *Music*—Music matters, and the key is cultural translation. And remember, there's no such thing as traditional music.
- *Building*—From the moment when *nones* first view the church and its grounds, the initial impression is made; physical surroundings convey strong messages.
- *Importance of the Visual*—Over the last twenty years we have decisively moved to a visually based world, and the church needs to move with it.

they had transformed a meager space into a time machine with special-effects music that took the kids back into Bible times. New kids, such as ours, were treated extra special and taken to a treasure chest full of small toys from which they could choose, just for coming the first time.

We went to some of the best churches in the area that summer, but our kids *pleaded* with us to take them back to the one we could barely stand.

Now, if I lived there and felt compelled to find a church home as a father of four, do you think I would have at least given that church another try? You can count on it. Most parents would.

Here's the lesson: You can drop the ball in the service, but ace it with the kids and you'll still have a chance that they will return. But no matter how good the service is, if the children's ministry is bad, they won't come back—unless they don't have kids.

Too many pastors treat children's ministry as a necessary evil. It's severely underfunded, understaffed, and underappreciated. Wake up. Children are the heart of your growth engine. If *nones* ever come to your church uninvited, it will probably be for the sake of their kids. And if *nones* come because they are invited, what you do with their children could be a deal breaker.

In other words, you live and die by the strength of your children's ministry. I know; you're thinking they shouldn't make such consumer decisions. But you're forgetting that they aren't Christ followers; all they have is consumerism. And meeting their needs in this way isn't compromising the gospel one bit. It's being strategic. And, I might add, it is bringing the message of the gospel, in age-appropriate ways, to the lives of those kids.

Music

I loved *Sister Act*. I know, it's really, really dated; but what a fun flick.

When the character played by Whoopi Goldberg, a "nun on the run" if there ever was one, puts contemporary music into the struggling parish's services, the crowds pour in. The priest, confronting the Mother Superior's concerns about such outlandish tunes, admonishes her by simply saying, "That music. That wonderful music. It *calls* to them."[6]

And music does. It always has.

Let's not get into the worship wars stuff. But let's *do* be savvy. There is no such thing as traditional music. All music was, at one time, newfangled, contemporary, cutting-edge, and probably too loud. The great hymns of Martin Luther are considered traditional and sacred to our ears, but they were anything *but* traditional and sacred to the people of Luther's day. Many of the great hymns written during the Protestant Reformation, such as "A Mighty Fortress Is Our God," were based on barroom tunes that were popular during that period. Luther simply changed the lyrics and then put the song into the life of the church. The result? People were able to meaningfully express themselves in worship—or at least connect with it stylistically.

Charles Wesley also borrowed from the secular music of his day, and John Calvin hired secular songwriters to put his theology to music, leading the Queen of England to call them "Geneva Jigs." Bach provides a similar pattern, as he used a popular form of music known as the cantata for weekly worship music. He was also known to seize tunes from "rather questionable sources and rework them for the church." Even Handel's *Messiah* was condemned as "vulgar theater" by the churchmen of his day for having too much repetition and not enough content.[7]

That last line is worth rereading. The point? Throughout history you'll find a connection between church growth and contemporary music. Sorry if that's too crass for you, but it's true. Don't ever downplay music—remember, there's an entire book of the Bible that is almost nothing but lyrics you can work from. So here are two words that will serve you well: *music matters*.

Just as the deeper issue with friendliness is an atmosphere of acceptance, the deeper issue with music is cultural translation. Let's retire such words as *relevant* and *contemporary*, shall we? The heart of it all is a missionary enterprise: learn the language of the people, the music, the dress, the customs—and then translate the gospel for them.

Chase this with me for a moment. If we were dropped into the deepest reaches of the Amazon basin as missionaries of the gospel to reach a specific unreached tribe of people, we would attempt to learn the language, dress in a way that is appropriate, craft a worship experience that uses indigenous instruments and styles, and work tirelessly to translate the Scriptures into their language. No one would argue with that approach. It's Missiology 101. Now realize that *your* mission field is the West. Are you doing the work of a missionary?

Building

As the familiar phrase goes, "You don't get a second chance at a first impression." Your guests' first impression begins long before the service ever does; it begins the moment they drive into the parking lot. It is at that moment—when they first view the church and its grounds—that the initial impression is made. Physical surroundings convey strong messages: if the lighting is inadequate, the message is *unfriendly*; if the equipment and facilities are out of date, the message is *irrelevant*; if the upkeep is poor, the message is *you haven't got it together*, or even worse, *this God you serve must not deserve better*.

So let's get real practical. What is the parking lot like? Are the stripes clearly painted, or are they faded with age? Is there trash strewn around? Are bushes and hedges trimmed? Is the grass neatly mowed? Is the church sign on the front lawn by the street in good shape, with letters neatly arranged with an appealing message or interesting information?

But physical surroundings includes far more than the external appearance of the facilities; they are the internal state of the facilities as well. Years ago when my wife and I moved from Louisville, Kentucky, to Nashville, Tennessee—having left the pastorate for a denominational position—our family experienced what was for us a rare and interesting phenomenon: church shopping. At the time, my wife and I had three young children. As you may guess, the room of greatest interest to us was the nursery.

We were stunned by what we found: sheets on cribs that hadn't been changed in weeks; paint peeling off the walls; toys in ridiculous disrepair and condition; poor lighting and ventilation; insufficient supervision. One church nursery was so bad that we could not in good conscience leave our youngest child in order to participate in the worship service. The church we eventually joined, however, was vastly different. The sheets were changed after every use; toys were in excellent condition and disinfected between sessions; a teacher-child ratio was provided that was more than adequate; there was excellent lighting and ventilation; the carpet was immaculately cleaned and vacuumed; security procedures were followed. We left our kids and said, "Here they are—we'll see you in six months!"

Just kidding. We picked them up in three.

The principle of cleanliness extends to all areas of the church, such as the restrooms, vestibule, classrooms, and of course, the front of the auditorium or sanctuary. I have been in numerous churches where the front part of the sanctuary, where the eyes of all in attendance are focused for an hour or more, was anything but impressive.

After a seminar I led on such issues, a pastor came to me and said he didn't think that he had ever sat in one of the pews in his church and examined the appearance of the front of the sanctuary. He later wrote me and shared that when he did, he was horrified at what he saw: hymnbooks strewn haphazardly all over the top of the piano and organ, old Sunday school quarterlies beside the pulpit, corners of the carpet frayed and worn, chipped wood on the furniture, and several burned-out light bulbs. He wrote, "To think that our visitors were staring at that mess for over an hour!"

It has been said that familiarity breeds inattention, and this is certainly true in terms of the physical appearance and cleanliness of our churches. If you discover a crack in the mirror of your bathroom, your immediate reaction is a resolve to see to its speedy repair. After a few busy weeks, you notice it again, and make a mental note to see that it receives attention. After six months, you simply don't see it anymore. But your guests *do*.

It brings to mind the time Ray Kroc, the founder of McDonald's, paid a surprise visit to a Winnipeg franchise. It is reported that he found a dead fly in a condiment jar. The franchisee lost his McDonald's franchise two weeks later.[8] Another tale of Kroc's commitment to cleanliness tells how on his way back to the office from lunch, Kroc asked his driver to pass through the parking lots of several McDonald's. In one of those parking lots, Kroc spotted some papers caught up in the shrubs along the outer fence. Immediately Kroc went to the nearest pay phone and called the office, got the name of the local manager, and then called him to offer his help in picking up the trash

in the parking lot. Later, both Ray Kroc and the young manager of
the restaurant met in the parking lot and got down on their hands and
knees to pick up the paper.[9] If that commitment exists in the secular
world for the sake of profit, how much more should the commitment
of God's people be for the sake of first impressions for the gospel?

Of course, as the other areas have deeper issues at play, so does
a building—as in what kind of building is best. Some may wonder
whether a traditional church-type building is important at all, if not
detrimental. Would it be better to invite a *none* to something less
intimidating, or more to the point, less *churchy*? If they have rejected
the idea of church and labels and denominations, could that setting
be best? Perhaps.

Many churches in the eighties began dropping denominational
labels from their name, becoming *community* churches. Now the move
is to drop the tag *church* altogether. So churches become "spiritual
communities" or "gatherings." This is now moving to how we think
about buildings. Rather than meet in traditional church buildings, the
preferred place to meet is a movie theater, community center, high
school, warehouse, or coffeehouse.

But even if you keep to the idea of a church building, is it best to
have the typical stained glass and pews? When we recently expanded
one of our campuses, we installed seating that was more like you
would find in a theater or performing arts center. Large atriums with
a bookstore and coffee shop were put in place, and the children's
ministry was upgraded with special one-way windows for parents
to see their children and decor with themes like you would find in a
children's store or children's park.

Does all this matter? It depends on whether or not you are expect-
ing company. We are.

The Importance of the Visual

The Lindisfarne Gospels, a 1,300-year-old manuscript, is revered to this
day as the oldest surviving English version of the Gospels. Lindisfarne
is a small island just off the Northumberland coast of England. It is
often referred to as Holy Island. Tidal waters cut it off from the rest

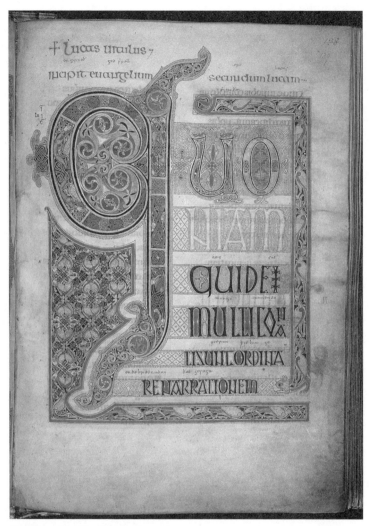

Page from the Lindisfarne Gospels

of the world for several hours every day, adding to its mystique as a spiritual pilgrimage.

Produced around AD 715 in honor of St. Cuthbert, largely by a man named Eadfrith, the Bishop of Lindisfarne, the Lindisfarne Gospels presents a copy of the four Gospels of the New Testament. But it isn't revered simply for its age. Its pages reveal curvy, embellished letters, strange creatures, and spiraling symbols of exquisite precision and beauty. During the eighth century, pilgrims flocked to St. Cuthbert's shrine where it was housed, making the Lindisfarne manuscript one of the most visited and seen books of its day. Its artwork and symbols helped convey its message to those who could not read.

Professor Richard Gameson from Durham University sees it as a precursor to modern multimedia because it was designed to be a visual, sensual, and artistic experience for its audience. Michelle Brown from the University of London notes that the book's impact was similar to those of films and electronic media today. As Gameson adds, "The emphasis was to reach as many people as possible."[10]

This is the final, and increasingly crucial, element to an open front door: *be visual.*

I have written in other places that there are striking parallels between our day and that of the Middle Ages.[11] But if we are entering a new era that is similar to the earlier medieval era, what does that mean? If we are following the medieval pattern—and I believe that in many ways we are—there will be at least five dynamics:

1. widespread spiritual illiteracy
2. indiscriminate spiritual openness
3. deep need for visual communication
4. attraction to spiritual experience
5. widespread ethos of amorality

That is why the term *neomedieval*, first offered by Umberto Eco in regard to Western society, seems appropriate.[12]

But it is the visual element that churches neglect to their peril. Over the last twenty years, we have decisively moved to a visually based world. The most formative influences are not books, theater, or even music. They are films.

Throw in videos and the rise of YouTube, and you have the essence of a cultural revolution—not to mention something of a return to the medieval. For example, during the Middle Ages there was widespread spiritual illiteracy, as well as actual illiteracy. People couldn't read.

This is why pilgrimages mattered so much to the pilgrims. Beyond the relics and holy places they thought might bestow grace, usually the cathedrals they visited held relics that told the story of faith through a medium they could understand: stained glass, pictures.

So while people couldn't, or didn't, read, they couldn't help but see, and from seeing, understand. It's no different today. We are spiritually illiterate and are visually oriented and visually informed. Only now, instead of stained glass, we have film. At Meck, there is very little we don't try to convey visually, whether it's a song during worship or a point during a message. It's simply how people best receive information and meaning, content and context. And because it is part of the arts, it has a way of sneaking past the defenses of the heart. And *nones* need a lot *snuck* past them.

Questions for Discussion and Reflection

1. Every church has a "front door," both literally and figuratively. So shouldn't they be opened in such a way as to strategically impact *nones* and other unchurched folks? How does your church currently do this?

2. Look again at this statistic: "of all unchurched people, 82 percent would come to church this weekend if they were invited by a friend." Ruminate on this. What can you do to capitalize on this at your church? What's stopping you from doing it now?

3. All churches think they're friendly. You probably think yours is. But is it friendly only to those already there, or is it just as friendly (or friendlier) to those who show up for the first time?

4. Creating that atmosphere of friendliness is really developing an atmosphere of acceptance. It's important to remember that if you want to reach the *nones*, they are going to come with all of their baggage. Will those people be treated with the love and respect they deserve, or will they be greeted with little grace and no acceptance?

5. When you start to see reaching the *nones* in this light, you start to understand that this kind of ministry is going to require you to get your hands dirty. Are you ready to make that kind of

commitment? Is the church you attend ready to have that vision cast?

6. Something much overlooked in service offerings is the children's ministry. This is craziness. What we need to understand is that the children's ministry is a deal breaker and a deal maker. If it's bad, you'll lose that family after the first visit. If it's good, you will probably get them back even if they didn't care for the message or other aspects of the church. If that's the case, does the children's ministry at your church receive the attention it deserves, both strategically and financially?

7. Music is a contentious issue for many congregations, especially those that have been around for quite some time. But one of the most important things to remember about music is that there is no such thing as traditional music. All music was at one time groundbreaking, culture shocking, or looked down on because it was new. But as you read earlier, you'll find a connection between church growth and contemporary music throughout history. Does your church offer music that helps you reach those far from God, or is it a barrier to someone who didn't grow up in church?

8. Your facility, building, grounds, and restrooms form the first impression for those who arrive at your church for the first time. Are you looking at it with the eyes of someone looking to find something wrong—someone who's never been to a church before?

13

Reimagining the Church

I've saved the most important for last. If the church is going to reach out to a group of people who have given up on the church, not to mention membership and labels, then one thing is clear: we must renew our own commitment to the very thing they have rejected—the church.

This is the enterprise that Jesus himself declared would be "so expansive with energy that not even the gates of hell will be able to keep it out" (Matt. 16:18 Message). Jesus made this staggering claim because the church would be his ongoing incarnation on planet Earth. It would be his body, his presence, his life. It would be the means for his ongoing ministry to the world. This is not simply as the universal body of believers around the world, but as concrete communities of faith gathered together in the name of Christ as mission outposts to the world. And it's needed.[1]

Reflecting on a lifetime of study in the social sciences, Peter Berger suggests that the key to resisting the secular culture of our day is for communities of faith to self-consciously and determinedly stand against its onslaught.[2] As critical as the process of secularization may be to understand, it pales in comparison with grasping the church's mandate to engage in the process of "counter-secularization." Famed missiologist Lesslie Newbigin would agree: "I have come to feel that the primary reality of which we have to take account in seeking for a Christian impact on public life is the Christian congregation. . . . [Jesus] did not write a book but formed a community."[3]

Steve Bruce gives the analogy of a garden in the midst of a wilderness, noting that "as the wilderness grows and the size of the cultivated area shrinks, the gardeners need to work harder."[4] We do not live and breathe in a neutral environment but in the midst of a hostile conflict, and we are behind enemy lines. The god of this world has been named, and he is firmly on his throne. There is only one domain beyond his control that stands in the way of total dominion. As a result, the body of Christ is under constant assault, for it stands alone against the night. It demands constant reinforcement and steadfast commitment. The church is not simply in the vanguard of kingdom advance, it is the entire assault force.

Ecclesiology 101

The word *church*, from the Greek word *ecclesia*, literally means "the called-out ones." It is a word that was used in Jesus's day for any group that was gathered together for a specific purpose or mission. Jesus seized the term to speak of a group with a specific purpose or mission, setting it apart from every other group or mission. This is where *ecclesiology*, the theological term for the doctrine of the church, finds its origin. The church of Christ, however, is anything but a man-made organization; instead it was founded and instituted by Jesus himself (Matt. 16:18).

The Bible has three primary understandings of this church, the body of Christ: (1) the local church, (2) the universal church as it exists around the world, and (3) the church as it exists throughout time and history, incorporating all of the saints that will one day be gathered together in heaven. Without question, the dominant biblical use is in reference to a local church or collection of local churches as defined bodies of believers that were gathered with both intent and order. Think of how the letters of Paul were written: "to the church of God in Corinth"; "to the churches in Galatia"; "to the church of the Thessalonians"; and at the beginning of John's Revelation, "to the seven churches in the province of Asia."

The local church was to serve as the ongoing manifestation of Christ himself on earth, being called his "body"—an idea of profound significance throughout the New Testament. As the apostle Paul writes:

> Just as each of us has one body with many members, and these members do not all have the same function, so in Christ we, though many, form one body, and each member belongs to all the others. We have different gifts, according to the grace given to each of us. (Rom. 12:4–6)

Later in the New Testament, Paul reiterates this idea: "Now you are the body of Christ, and each one of you is a part of it" (1 Cor. 12:27). And if the point hadn't been made clearly enough, Paul writes the following words to the church at Ephesus: "And God placed all things under his feet and appointed him to be head over everything for the church, which is his body, the fullness of him who fills everything in every way" (Eph. 1:22–23; see also 5:23; Col. 1:18, 2:19). Beyond the interconnectedness this suggests, it means that the church is the locus of Christ's activity and he works through the church now as he worked through his physical body during his thirty-three-year life. In the New Testament there is *no* ministry outside of the church, or at least its umbrella.

But what is this *local* church that functions as the body of Christ?

One, Holy, Catholic, Apostolic

During the next few centuries, the church defined itself by four very important words: (1) *one*, (2) *holy*, (3) *catholic*, and (4) *apostolic*.[5] Each word carries great significance. First, as we explored in an earlier chapter, the church was to be *one*, or unified. Jesus, in his great and grand final prayer recorded in John's Gospel, prayed fervently for unity among those of us who would embrace his name in years and centuries to come. Second, it was to be a *holy* church, meaning set apart for God and separate from the world, for God himself is holy. The church was to reflect this holiness to the degree that it can be identified with God as holy. Third, the church was to be *catholic*, which simply means universal. The church was meant to be a worldwide church that includes all believers under its umbrella. So the word *catholic* was used of the church long before any kind of institution within Christianity used it for its own. Finally, the church was to be *apostolic*, which means committed to the teaching handed down by Jesus through the apostles.

Beyond being one, holy, catholic, and apostolic, local churches were entities that had definition and form, structure and purpose. They were not simply doing *community* in the broadest sense, much less simply pursuing ministry. In the Bible, the church was a defined, purposeful gathering of believers who knew they were coming together to *be* a church. There were defined entry and exit points to the church; clear theological guidelines navigating corporate and community waters; the responsibility of stewarding the sacraments; specifically named leadership positions; and, of course, a singular mission. One often hears that the church is where "the Gospel is rightly taught and the sacraments rightly administered." This is taken from the Augsburg Confession (1530), the primary confessional statement of the Lutheran church courtesy of Martin Luther and Philipp Melanchthon. Calvin said much the same thing in his *Institutes*.[6] But sensing the inadequacy of such a definition, in 1539 Luther wrote *On the Councils and the Church*, adding five more distinguishing characteristics, including church discipline, ordination, and worship through prayer and singing.

The Bible speaks of defined organizational roles such as pastors, elders, bishops, and deacons, as well as corporate roles related to spiritual gifts such as teachers, administrators, and of course, leaders (see Romans 12; 1 Corinthians 12; Ephesians 4; 1 Peter 4). These corporate dynamics allowed money to flow from one group to another

One, Holy, Catholic, Apostolic

- One: the church was to be one, or unified
- Holy: the church was to be set apart for God and separate from the world, for God himself is holy
- Catholic: the church was meant to be a worldwide church that includes all believers under its umbrella
- Apostolic: the church was to be committed to the teaching handed down by Jesus through the apostles

(see 2 Corinthians 8); decisions to be made by leaders as to doctrine and practice (see Acts 15); and the setting apart of some individuals for appointed tasks, mission, and church plants (see Acts 13). Paul talks of those "inside" the church and those "outside the church," and he speaks of the importance of expelling those who are wicked and unrepentant (1 Cor. 5:12–13), intimating membership or at least official associations.

There are often disparaging quips made about *organized religion*, but there was nothing *disorganized* about the biblical model. Those who intimate that the idea of the church in the New Testament is either so embryonic or so ethereal that there is a license to define the church in any way desired are simply misguided or misinformed.

Radical Revisionism

Tragically, Christ followers are notorious for being dismissive of the church, as if it is a disposable institution created by human beings as an option on the Christian front rather than the front itself—particularly among evangelical Christians. And no wonder.

Carl F. H. Henry, the founding editor of *Christianity Today* magazine, wrote a masterful six-volume systematic theology that set the stage for evangelical thinking for his generation. *God, Revelation and Authority*[7] insightfully explores the nature of theology and theological method; revelation, inspiration, and the canon of Scripture; and the existence and attributes of God, including the Trinity. It pursues issues related to creation and providence; human nature; as well as original and actual sin. It moved on to investigate the person and work of Christ, predestination, conversion, justification, sanctification and the work of the Holy Spirit, perseverance, and in the end, eschatology. Every major doctrine save one: the church.

Six volumes, the summa of evangelical thought, and not a single section on ecclesiology. This is nothing against Carl Henry; I studied under him as a graduate student, and he was a gracious and generous man, and we became friends. But he didn't seem to have a vision for the church. Few American evangelicals have. Not simply because our theologians have not led us, but because our enterprising spirit has numbed us to the *primacy* of the church—particularly through the explosion of the parachurch movement, aptly described as "religion gone entrepreneurial."[8] Missions and ministries, crusades and campaigns litter the American religious landscape—most without relation to the local church. Embraced as a way to enlarge the boundaries of God's work beyond the traditional church, for many it has become a substitute entity, often competitive and occasionally antagonistic.

To celebrate this as a paradigm shift from being church-centered to kingdom-centered is terrible theology. The church is *the* divinely instituted and appointed vehicle of kingdom ministry. The very meaning of the word *parachurch* is "that which is to come alongside [*para*] the church." It does not mean *beyond* the church, as some have suggested, just as the word *paracletos* for the Holy Spirit does not mean "beyond us" but "beside us" as Helper or Advocate.[9] Misunderstanding the nature and role of the parachurch has led some to actually speak of the "potential partnership" of the church and parachurch, as if it could be a nice option.[10] This devaluation of the church in terms of theology, attitude, commitment, and participation is a startling compromise of Christ's vision and intent. So let it be said that the church is not optional for the Christ follower; there is no ministry found in the New Testament that is not firmly planted under its canopy.

But that is not what others are saying, much less believing.

Near the beginning of my rather short tenure as a seminary president, I sat in the boardroom of a prominent Christian business leader to try to pitch a vision for contributing to theological education, specifically student scholarships. Instead of listening to the opportunity or asking pertinent questions as to the value of such an investment, he was determined to boast of his company's identity as a Christian enterprise. He told of the mission trips he had taken with his employees, the investments the company had made from its profits in select boutique parachurch ventures, and the Bible study offered on campus for employees. Throughout his self-congratulatory spiel he took more than his fair share of shots at local churches and pastors who were not as "alive" as he and his company were in their faith. Forgive me, but he was insufferably full of his own spiritual self-importance and virtue, as if he had drunk a bit too deeply from the fawning of countless pilgrims who had come to his corporate offices to laud his beneficence and ask for his generosity.

At the time, as a new seminary president facing an inherited budgetary shortfall of over one million dollars, I was willing to endure almost anything—or anyone—for aid. I smiled and nodded, affirming his many self-ascribed accolades. Then in the midst of one of his personal asides about the sorry state of the church as compared to the pristine missional nature of his business, he maintained that it was for this reason that he wasn't involved in a local church. They were, he intimated, beneath his own theological vision. "And after all," he added, "we're the church too."

Everything within me wanted to leap from my seat and shout, "Enough! No, you are *not!*" A company is *not* the body of Christ instituted as the hope of the world by Jesus himself, chronicled breathtakingly by Luke through the book of Acts, and shaped in thinking and practice by the apostle Paul through letter after letter as divinely preserved in the New Testament. A marketplace venture that offers itself on the New York Stock Exchange is not the entity that is so expansive with energy that not even the gates of hell can withstand its onslaught. An assembly of employees in cubicles working for end-of-year stock options and bonuses is not the gathering of saints bristling with the power of spiritual gifts as they mobilize to provide justice for the oppressed, service to the widow and the orphan, and compassion for the poor.

But it is not surprising that an evangelical, Bible-believing follower of Christ would think that it is. The research of D. Michael Lindsay on the leaders of evangelical Christianity found that among Christian presidents and CEO's, senior business executives and Hollywood icons, celebrated artists and world-class athletes, more than half had low levels of commitment to their congregations. Some were members in name only; others had actively disengaged from church life.[11]

With jaw-dropping vigor, ignorance, and at times unblushing gall, increasing sectors of the evangelical world are abandoning two thousand years of ecclesiology as if the church is some malleable human construct that can be shaped, altered, redefined, or even disposed of as desired. This, coupled with a radical revisionism in terms of biblical interpretation and ecclesial history that would seem more in line with *The Da Vinci Code* than Christian theology, the doctrine of the church is being reformulated apart from biblical moorings, or simply dismissed as if not a part of biblical orthodoxy at all. How can we blame the *nones* for doing any less?

Primacy for the Christian Life

The critical importance of the church goes well beyond strategic primacy. The church is decisive for the Christian to fulfill the Christian *life*. Consider what has been entrusted to the church for the sake of the Christian: the very confession of the gospel through proclamation; corporate worship; the stewarding of the sacraments; the dynamics of the new community in Christ; the use of and benefit from spiritual gifts; and spiritual care and protection through pastors. If you say this is meant to be afforded to us outside of the church, you haven't read the New Testament.

Far beyond the church's central role as the means by which this world is to be engaged and transformed, the church is the very body of Christ, one that every member of his body is meant to embrace. So penetrating was this understanding at the beginning of the Christian movement that it led the early church father Tertullian to maintain, "It is not possible to have God as Father without having the Church as mother." Saint Cyprian echoed this sentiment with the dictum, "*Nulla salus extra eclesiam*" ("apart, or outside, the church, there is no salvation"). As Philip D. Kenneson writes, "To be a Christian is inseparable from what it means to be the church."[12]

Idea and Ideal

I know that many, if not most, Christians have become disillusioned with the church.[13] As Katie Galli once noted about her fellow twenty-somethings, "We're disillusioned about almost everything—government, war, the economy. . . . We're *especially* disillusioned with the church. Somewhere between the Crusades, the Inquisition, and fundamentalists bombing abortion clinics, we lost our appetite for institutionalized Christianity."[14] I understand.

But it is an institution, and needs to be. And while "the church can indeed be bureaucratic, inefficient, and, at times, hopelessly outdated," Galli wisely adds, "it has also given us a 2,000-year legacy of saints and social reformers, and a rich liturgy and theology—the very gift twentysomethings need to grow into the full stature of Christ."[15] But this is far from a generational challenge. Baby boomer Philip Yancey writes of his estrangement from the church, noting how the hypocrisy of the members and the cultural irrelevance of its experience kept him away for years. Why did he return? "Christianity is not a purely intellectual, internal faith. It can only be lived in community."[16]

Ironically, the real dilemma facing the church is not the church itself but the staggering power of the biblical vision *for* the church. Christ's dream for the church is so strong, so compelling, so vibrant that the pale manifestations on the corner of Elm and Vine can breed disdain. As Sarah Cunningham writes, "I have been and continue to be frustrated when Christian religious systems seem to fall short of the community God intended his followers to experience. However, my belief in the ideal of church—in God's design for those who align themselves with him—is uncompromised."[17] But the telling statement comes later when she owns the rampant idealism that pervades her generation's approach to all of life: "It's no surprise, then, that twentysomethings tend to apply these same idealistic ideas to a search for the perfect church. When we don't find perfection, we can start to get a bit antsy."[18]

Any ideal can act in one of two ways: (1) it can drive you toward its fulfillment, or (2) it can drive you away from its pursuit entirely in disappointment. Sadly, many are choosing to leave the vision in disappointment. They remain loyal to the *idea* of church but not its practice, citing the chasm between the vision and the reality as their rationale. But this is precisely what must not happen.

Theologian Jürgen Moltmann reminds us that the church does not *have a mission*; rather, the mission *has us*. And it is the mission of Christ that creates the church.[19] God has sent himself, and he now sends us. This is the *missio dei*, the "sending of God." Or as Christopher J. H. Wright contends, our mission "means our committed participation as God's people, at God's invitation and command, in God's own mission within the history of God's world for the redemption of God's creation."[20] So to engage the mission of God is to engage his church; they are inextricably intertwined.

A Final Word

In his book *Courageous Leadership*, my friend Bill Hybels talks about having a defining moment on the place of church in his life.[21] It was the mid-1980s. He'd been out of the country for several weeks on a speaking trip and was returning to the U.S. through San Juan, Puerto Rico. He'd been outside of CNN range for most of the trip, so at the airport he was eager to grab a cup of coffee and a copy of *USA Today* and catch up.

Then it began. Two young boys—who looked like brothers—started squabbling with each other. The older kid appeared to be seven or eight, the younger one around five. Bill watched them a few seconds over the top of his paper, kind of irritated at how they were disturbing him and everyone else. But he said to himself, *Boys will be boys.*

Then he heard it. *Whack!*

He put down his paper because it was obvious that the older boy had just slapped his younger brother—*hard*—right across the face. The smaller boy was crying, and you could already see a nasty welt rising on his cheek. Bill looked around for a parent or two—anybody responsible for these kids who could stop the mayhem.

Then the entire gate area was silenced by a sound that none of them would forget for a very long time. It was the sound of a closed fist smashing into a face. While the little boy was still crying from the first slap, the older boy wound up and belted him again, literally knocking the little guy off his feet.

That was more than Bill could take. He blurted out, "Where are these kids' parents?"

No response.

As he raced over to the boys, the older boy grabbed the little guy by the hair and started pounding his face into the tile floor. *Bam! Bam! Bam!*

Bill then heard the final boarding call for his flight, but he was too sickened by the fight to abandon his mission. He grabbed the older boy by the arm and hauled him off the younger one, then he held them as far apart as he could. With one arm extending out to a kid with a bloody face and the other straining to stop a boy with murder in his eyes, he knew he was holding a human tragedy in his hands. Just then the ticket agent came up and said, "If you're Mr. Hybels, you've got to board this plane immediately. It's leaving now!" Reluctantly, he loosed his hold on the boys, gathered his things, and rushed down the gangplank, shouting out to the ticket agent, "Keep those kids apart! Please! And find their parents!"

He stumbled onto the plane and managed to find his seat, but he was badly shaken by what had happened. He couldn't get the sights and sounds of the violence he had witnessed between those two young boys out of his head. He grabbed a magazine and tried to read, but he couldn't concentrate. Then he looked in the entertainment magazine to see what movie was going to be shown, hoping it would be something that could distract his thinking. But then he sensed the Holy Spirit telling him not to purge his mind so quickly. He sensed a prompting:

Think about what you saw. Consider the implications. Let your heart be gripped by this reality.

So he did. He began to dwell on what he had seen, and his mind became flooded with thoughts about the older kid's life. He wondered where his parents were. He wondered what kind of experience he was having in school. He wondered if there was anybody in his life offering him love, guidance, and hope. He wondered what the boy's future held.

If he's throwing fists at the age of eight, what will he be throwing at eighteen? Knives? Bullets?

Where will he end up? In a nice house with a good wife and a satisfying job? Or in a jail cell, or an early grave?

Then Bill felt prompted to consider what could change the trajectory of that boy's life. He scrolled through the options. *Maybe*, he thought, *if we elect some really great government officials who will pass new legislation, maybe that will help a kid like this.* But will it?

No doubt, what governments do is very important. Writing legislation for the good of a society is a noble and worthy task. But politicians, no matter how sincere their motivation, can only do so much. They can rearrange the yard markers on the playing field of life, but they can't change a human heart. They can't heal a wounded soul. They can't turn hatred into love. They can't bring about repentance, forgiveness, reconciliation, or peace. They can't get to the core problem of the kid Bill saw in the airport and the millions of others like him.

Bill began to scroll through every option he could think of. Businessmen can provide sorely needed jobs. Wise educators can teach useful knowledge of the world. Self-help programs can offer some occasional methods of behavior modification. Advanced psychological techniques can aid self-understanding. And all of that is good—but can any of it truly transform the human heart? No.

Then it came to him like never before: Only one power exists on this planet that can do that. It's the power of the love of Jesus Christ, the love that conquers sin and wipes out shame and heals wounds and reconciles enemies and patches broken dreams, and ultimately changes the world, one life at a time. And the radical message of that transforming love has been given to the *church*. That is why the church is the most beautiful, the most radical, the most dangerous, the most glorious enterprise on the planet. There is nothing more worthy of throwing our lives into.

This is how Bill gathers his final thoughts:

> There is nothing like the local church when it's working right. Its beauty is indescribable. Its power is breathtaking. Its potential is unlimited. It comforts the grieving and heals the broken in the context of community. It builds bridges to seekers and offers truth to the confused. It provides resources for those in need and opens its arms to the forgotten, the downtrodden, the disillusioned. It breaks the chains of addictions, frees the oppressed, and offers belonging to the marginalized of this world. Whatever the capacity for human suffering, the church has a greater capacity for healing and wholeness.[22]

This is what we have been called to give our lives to, and in order to change the world, we *must* give our lives to it. Until we have this vision coursing through our veins, we will never be able to cast it before a watching world of *nones* who dismiss it as irrelevant at best and harmful at worst.

Questions for Discussion and Reflection

1. The church is spurned in many ways these days, even among Christians. But it will take a renewed and reimagined approach to church for us to reach the *nones*. The church is inseparable from the mission and teaching of Jesus. As missiologist Lesslie Newbigin notes, Jesus "did not write a book but formed a community."[23] That community is the assault force for the kingdom of God in this world. Do you think of the church like this? Do you need to reinvigorate your vision of what church is doing here on earth?

2. The local church is the very body of Christ manifested to serve his cause. It is connected to Jesus in a way nothing else is, which means no other manifestation of Christ can be as effective and as powerful in the march against hell as the church. Is this the notion you wake up with each morning? Is it the feeling you get when Sunday morning comes?

3. The local church is to be *one*, *holy*, *catholic*, and *apostolic*. *One* is the sense of being unified, as we read about in an earlier chapter. Is your local church embodying that call to unity?

4. The church is to be *holy*, meaning set apart so that the world will see the very holiness of God represented in the church itself. Will the world see the holiness of God reflected in your church body?

5. The church is meant to be *catholic*, which simply means universal or worldwide in scope and including all believers. Is your church part of the larger church of believers? Does it alienate, isolate, or insulate itself from the rest of the believers?

6. The church is to be *apostolic*, or devoted to the teaching of Jesus handed down by the apostles. Is this commitment to the teachings handed down by Jesus evident in your own teachings or the ways that you've been taught?

7. Beyond being *one*, *holy*, *catholic*, and *apostolic*, the church has always had definition, structure, and purpose. The biblical model of the church was never disorganized. Do you have a structure that is built to allow ministry to thrive in your community?

8. Have you been viewing the church and its existence, form, and substance as something open to interpretation? Are there any examples in the New Testament of ministry being done outside the canopy of the church?

Afterword

In *The Lord of the Rings*, J. R. R. Tolkien writes of a race of ancient tree shepherds called the Ents. In the midst of the war between good and evil engulfing Middle-earth, the Ents are insular, worrying more about their lost Entwives. Many have fallen so deeply asleep that it is not clear whether they will ever reawaken. Young hobbits Merry and Pippin begin a relationship with the leader of the Ents, Treebeard, and do everything they can to open his eyes to the needs of the world in light of its great conflict. The hobbits are somewhat successful in their efforts, and Treebeard gathers together the few remaining mobile Ents for an Entmoot to discuss the matter.

The Ents are maddeningly slow and methodical. After days of convening, Treebeard breaks away to give the hobbits an update. Hoping to hear about their decision to go to war against the forces of the Dark Lord Sauron, all Treebeard reports is that they have decided that hobbits should be added to the accepted list of other known creatures.

In the movie version, only when Treebeard sees the carnage enacted by the evil wizard Saruman against the forest does he bypass the slowness inherent in his race, call the Ents to action, and go to war. As Gandalf the wizard had earlier predicted, if the Ents awakened, they would discover they were strong. And they were.

I am reminded of this scene often in relation to the rise of the *nones*. Personally, I am not surprised by the many findings revealed in this book. It's just the latest manifestation of a cultural trajectory we've been on and that I've been charting for some time.

But I am grateful. Why? Because I pray it will be the desperately needed wake-up call for American Christianity—a wake-up call to shake us from the trivial and divisive, the mundane and the meaningless. This is no time for such things. The need is too urgent, the day too dark, and the challenge too great.

This is no time for cross-town church competitions for transfer growth and then patting ourselves on the back for reaching the already convinced as if we somehow made a dent in hell.

This is no time to cling to outdated forms of communication or style because of the fear of change—not to mention the selfish attitudes we turn into theological fences we then build around our personal taste.

This is no time to cave in to spiritual narcissism, in which the primary concern is whether people are fed, are ministered to, or "get anything out of the worship experience," as though the mission is caring for believers as consumers instead of dying to ourselves to reach a lost world.

This is no time for seminaries and their leaders to bow down in front of the academy, as if the ultimate goal is getting another paper into another academic journal on some inane issue irrelevant to anyone but fellow academics, when students are in desperate need to be trained and developed to lead churches to their fullest redemptive potential.

This is no time to keep putting evangelism down in the name of discipleship as if spending energy on one takes away from spending energy on the other, thus falsely spiritualizing a passive approach to outreach.

This is no time for denominations to protect outdated programs, agencies, policies, or strategies that no longer work—continuing to foist them onto churches in the name of effectiveness, self-preservation, and revenue stream.

This is no time to wave the flag of social ministry and justice issues so single-mindedly in the name of cultural acceptance and the hip factor that it becomes our collective substitute for the clear articulation of the gospel.

In other words, this is no time to wander around looking for Ent-wives or spend time worrying about how to classify hobbits.

It's time to wake up and engage the battle at hand. And that battle is clear: we must do whatever it takes, barring any reduction of the gospel itself, to bring this world to Christ. The rise of the *nones* will only continue. Our only hope, and the heart of the Great Commission, is to stem the tide by turning the *nones* into *wons*.

And it can happen. Sociologists Roger Finke and Rodney Stark write that at the time of the American Revolution, only about one-fifth of Americans could be considered "churched." By the time of the Civil War, that number had increased to one-third. Today it is more than half. Granted, the genesis of this book is how that trend is now reversed, but the climb in involvement throughout early American history can be recaptured. "The churching of America," Finke and Stark offer, "was accomplished by aggressive churches committed to vivid otherworldliness."[1]

If we make that same commitment again, we may just find—as did the Ents—that we are strong.

Appendix A

Judged

The following is the transcription of a talk titled "Judgmentalism" that was delivered at Mecklenburg Community Church in 2012. It was the first installment of a series simply titled "Judged." The intent was to address the perception among the *nones* that Christians are judgmental as well as the actual experiences some of them have had of being judged. The lead-in to the talk itself was a video produced by Worship House Media, also titled "Judged," which can be viewed at www.worshiphousemedia.com/mini-movies/27317/Judged.

□ □ □

Introduction

Rejected.
Crushed.
Shunned.
Hurt.
Cast out.
Unloved.
Because of the way they look, the things they've done, the questions they've asked, the mistakes they've made.

Judged.

By the very people they hoped would help them, accept them, get them back on their feet. People who call themselves Christians.

And it made them turn away, turn off, and tune out.

If that's church, if that's Christianity, you can count them out.

Ever felt that way? I'll bet you have.

Judgmentalism

David Kinnaman and Gabe Lyons did a major study on people who had turned away from the Christian faith in a book called *UnChristian*. Biggest reason? When people who had given up on church and faith thought of Christians, all that came to mind was a bunch of people who were judgmental.

Prideful, acting morally superior, and from that, finding fault with everybody else.

People who lacked compassion, lacked understanding, and lacked grace toward other people's screw-ups.

People who seemed more interested in condemning others than helping people.

So for instance, a single mother comes to a church looking for community and support, wanting to find God. She's not proud she got pregnant. It wasn't her plan A for doing life. But it happened, and she's alone. So she turns to God's people, hoping for a second chance. What do you think she'll hear?

"You shouldn't be a single mother. Shame on you."

Or other examples:

You shouldn't be an addict.

You shouldn't be divorced.

You shouldn't drink.

You shouldn't be living together.

You shouldn't be attracted to people of the same sex.

You shouldn't have questions.

Bad, terrible, horrible you. You have no business being here among us "good" people.

Philip Yancey tells a story about a friend of his who works with the down-and-out in Chicago. A prostitute came to him in about as bad shape as you can be. She was homeless, her health was failing, and she wasn't able to buy food for her two-year-old daughter. In fact, with tears streaming down her face, she confessed that she had been renting out her daughter to men in order to support her drug habit. Yancey's friend could hardly bear to hear the details. He sat in silence, not even knowing what to say. But in the end, he asked her if she had ever thought of going to a church for help. And he said he will never forget the look of pure astonishment that crossed her face. "Church!" she said. "Why would I ever go there? They'd just make me feel even worse than I already do!"[1]

And when she and others like her are asked why they feel that way, why they think that would be the reception, the answer is always the same: Because it happened to me.

Experience. Firsthand knowledge. Is that your story? Do people who need help feel from past experience that if they ever fell flat on their face, shipwrecked their life, screwed things up so royally that they couldn't see daylight, that the last place they'd go running to would be God's people?

Well, even if you don't have that in your past—you know they would be right. A lot of churches, and a lot of Christians, are everything they fear and hate.

When it comes to their desire for grace,

> that incredible commodity that sees us for who we really are, not just for our mistakes and failures and flaws,
>
> that dispenser of forgiveness,
>
> that spirit that restores those who have fallen,
>
> that one who is so *amazing* that we sing songs called "Amazing Grace,"
>
> that powerful force unleashed on this planet by Jesus himself,

. . . often the last place it's found is with Jesus's people.

Don't Judge

So what happened? It's simple. We've stopped being like Jesus—because he went out of his way to tell those who followed him not to judge!

Did you know that? Listen to his words from the most famous talk he ever gave—what's called the Sermon on the Mount:

> Do not judge, or you too will be judged. For in the same way you judge others, you will be judged, and with the measure you use, it will be measured to you.
>
> Why do you look at the speck of sawdust in your brother's eye and pay no attention to the plank in your own eye? How can you say to your brother, "Let me take the speck out of your eye," when all the time there is a plank in your own eye? You hypocrite, first take the plank out of your own eye, and then you will see clearly to remove the speck from your brother's eye. (Matt. 7:1–5)

That's quite clear, isn't it? Jesus said, "Do not judge." Period. That's God's job, not ours.

Now, it's very important to understand what Jesus means by judging others. It doesn't mean we can never make a value judgment. Some things are wrong; some things are right.

This isn't about never taking a stand. It isn't about being a moral wimp. Some people think acceptance means mindless affirmation. Validating everything—every choice, every lifestyle. That's stupid.

If someone came up to me and said, "I believe that the best way for you to optimize the performance of your laptop is to,

remove your antivirus protection,

take down your firewall,

open up every email attachment from people and companies you do not know,

download as much free software as you can from sites you have never heard of,

and respond to that long-lost Nigerian uncle who just left you ten million dollars and all he needs from you is your bank account number and password

I would say, "That is the stupidest thing I've ever heard." Is that being judgmental? Of course not.

It's not about refusing to believe something, hold to something, or stand for something.

It's not about refusing to say you feel something is right or wrong, good or bad.

It's not about giving up thinking, or discernment, or wisdom.

It's not about never warning someone.

If someone I care about is living in a way that is destroying his or her life and I don't say anything to him or her, I don't love that person very much. If someone can't see where he or she is walking and is about to step off a cliff, it's not judgmental to say, "Stop!"

It's not judgmental to tell someone reaching for a bottle of Visine for dry eyes that it is actually a bottle of carbolic acid. That's not being judgmental; that's caring enough for someone to tell him or her the truth.

So what is judgmentalism? Judgmentalism is the practice of personal condemnation. John Stott puts it this way: the judgmental person Jesus is talking about is someone who "is a fault-finder who is negative and destructive towards other people and enjoys actively seeking out their failings. He puts the worst possible construction of their motives, pours cold water on their [dreams], and is ungenerous toward their mistakes."[2]

A judgmental person makes sweeping assessments of other people. A judgmental person assigns them the worst possible motives without any real knowledge of what's going on in their life or their context or their situation. A judgmental person has a pounce-and-denounce kind of demeanor.

If you are judgmental, you make yourself out to be God and take on God's role as Judge. That's why Jesus said that if you judge others, you will be judged, because the heart of a judgmental attitude is to assume yourself to be so morally superior that you can take over God's role in someone else's life.

Jesus says, "Fine—if you do that, then expect to be judged by those standards." God will judge you on the basis of whether you measure up to the standard required for judging—which is being God yourself.

Anybody want to go through that test? I don't, because I'm not God, and if I get judged like I am, it's going to be *epic fail* time. Instead, I need to see myself the way I am:

a fellow screw-up
a fellow struggler
a fellow sinner

Look at how this is talked about in the New Testament book of Romans:

You may be saying, "What terrible people . . . !" But wait a minute! You are just as bad. When you say they are wicked and should be punished, you are [condemning] yourselves, for you do these very same things. . . . Don't you realize how patient [God] is being with you? . . . Can't you see that he has been waiting all this time without punishing you, to give you time to turn from your sin? (Rom. 2:1, 4 TLB)

So why do we do it? Well, one reason is that we are quick to take offense. Really, it's like we've got a chip on our shoulder. We are so hypersensitive to other people and what they may do against us, or we disagree with or don't like what they are doing.

You know, I'm going to be very candid in this series and share a lot of stories with you. And I remember one from a few years back.

Those of you who know my wife, Susan, know she is one of the kindest, sweetest, gentlest people on this planet. Well, there was a woman who got angry with her and wrote her a terrible note as to why she was angry. Here was her reason: "When you stopped me in the hall today and asked me how I was doing and said you had been praying for me and that you cared about me and you hugged me, well, you didn't hug me long enough."

"You didn't hug me long enough"? I thought, *Wow. What is up with that kind of judgmental spirit?*

Another reason we rush to judgment with people? Let me tell you another story.

Back when I was in seminary, I was pastor of a little county-seat church outside of town. The church was very small, and the staff was basically—well, me.

One day a woman called up and asked for some help from the church because she was sick and had a lot of bills. So I went over to visit her and brought another woman from the church with me, to help me assess the situation.

When we showed up at the house, I remember thinking that this woman's hair looked perfect. It was done up so fancy that it looked like she had just come from what in those days we called the *beauty parlor*. It looked really good—like expensive good.

Then as we walked into the house with her there was a door open to her room, and there on a shelf were some really, really nice-looking wigs. Again, expensive-looking wigs.

After talking for a bit, we left, and I said to the woman who had come with me, "Those were some nice wigs."

She said, "*Really* nice wigs. Those were expensive."

I instantly thought *Man, she doesn't need any help. If she can afford to spend money on those wigs, then she's just looking for a handout and trying to hit on the church.*

Well, I later found out that the woman had cancer and that part of her treatment involved chemotherapy. She had lost all of her hair, and a loving friend had purchased the wigs for her so she wouldn't have to go around bald.

Sadly, that woman had a pastor who was a jerk because of a rush to judgment.

Why We Judge (Don't Be a Hypocrite)

Do you know what's the biggest reason that we judge others? Because it makes us feel better about ourselves. We act morally superior because we *like* feeling morally superior. That's why we minimize our own faults and failures and exaggerate somebody else's. It makes us feel better about ourselves. It's how we build ourselves up.

When we highlight the way somebody else is screwing up and condemn them, we feel better about our own screwups. Then we can act like we don't have any.

There's a word for that: *hypocrisy*. The word *hypocrite* literally means "mask wearer." It's a Greek term that comes from Greek theater.

Greek actors held up a mask and spoke from behind it. The mask was the *hypocrite*.

So religious hypocrites are people who deliberately set out to deceive other people about who they are. They live life behind a mask. Their spirituality is theater—make-believe, a role they're playing for others. And the heart of the act is elevating themselves as if they are righteous, and tearing other people down as if they are the bad guys.

But when the mask falls and we see who these hypocrites really are, what do we find out? They are doing the very same things they condemn other people for doing:

> the guy who condemned homosexuality is hooking up with guys,
>
> the person who condemned porn is addicted to porn,
>
> the person who said "don't sleep around" is sleeping around.

That's why Jesus hates hypocrisy so much. Take another look:

> Why do you look at the speck of sawdust in your brother's eye and pay no attention to the plank in your own eye? How can you say to your brother, "Let me take the speck out of your eye," when all the time there is a plank in your own eye? You hypocrite, first take the plank out of your own eye. (Matt. 7:3–5)

All Sinners

I mentioned Philip Yancey earlier. In his book *What's So Amazing About Grace*, he makes a telling observation. He notes that with Jesus, there were only two categories of people: (1) sinners who admit it, and (2) sinners who deny it. Sinners who admit it receive his grace, compassion, and forgiveness. Sinners who don't get the very judgment they are dealing out on others. Or as many have observed, Jesus came to comfort the afflicted and afflict the comfortable.

So get this one straight: the Christian life isn't about pretending you have it all together when you don't.

It reminds me of something Will Campbell wrote. Known for his disarmingly earthy approach to spirituality and life, he was asked this question: "In ten words or less, what's the Christian message? . . . Let me have it. Ten words."

He said, "We're all bastards but God loves us anyway."[3] And he was right.

If Christianity is about anything, it's about serious imperfection that desperately needs forgiveness and grace. It's not having our act together—it's admitting that we don't! Then it's about coming to Christ for a relationship built on grace and forgiveness, and then becoming who we were meant to be.

So let me set something straight right here and now that you may have never heard before: this church is led by a sinner. Come spend a day with me and I guarantee I will disappoint you. I love my wife, but you will see how I fail daily in being the husband I'm supposed to be. I love my four children, but you will witness the countless times I am insensitive and impatient.

And those are just the easy ones to admit. I love God and urge others to do the same, but if you want to see someone who fails to consistently live in light of what he knows about how he *ought* to live, I'm your man.

But the truth runs even deeper. As a Christ follower, I remain a sinner who struggles with sin and often loses.

But all Christians do.

I remember reading something about the life of Alexander Whyte, a Christian leader in nineteenth-century Scotland. He was once approached by a woman who showered praise on him and his life. You know what he said to her? "Madam, if you knew the man I really was, you would spit in my face."

But does that mean that all Christians are counterfeits? Or that the Christian life and faith are meaningless? No!

I screw up a thousand times a day, but I'm more like Jesus now than I was five years ago in so many areas of my life. And the life I would be living apart from Christ is almost unthinkable.

We've all got the same sickness, and we're all in the same hospital for treatment. Some are further along the path of recovery than others, and some are better at following the prescribed treatment than others. But we all have the same disease. We're all being treated for sin-sickness. We're all in some kind of recovery.

So whatever baggage you brought with you today, you're not alone. And we do not condemn you.

You are no different than any of the rest of us struggling with areas of temptation and desire. We've all failed in those areas. But Christ is working on all of us.

Mecklenburg Community Church is nothing but a colossal collection of moral foul-ups. Really—you're in some bad company here. We have sins of pride, greed, pornography, self-righteousness, lying, stealing, adultery, insensitivity to others. But through the power of Christ, there is hope for all of us.

But here's what else you need to know: we want to expose these areas in our life, not deny them or rationalize them away. Not in a way that condemns, but in a way that transforms. We want to discover them, go to God for forgiveness, and become increasingly changed people.

The Church

Someone sent me something about how one church decided to make this as clear as possible. Here's what they have in their program each week:

> We extend a special welcome to those who are single, married, divorced . . . filthy rich, dirt poor, *no habla ingles.* . . .
>
> You're welcome here if you're just browsing, just woke up, or just got out of jail.
>
> We welcome soccer moms, NASCAR dads, starving artists, tree-huggers, latte-sippers, vegetarians, junk-food eaters.
>
> We welcome those who are in recovery or still addicted.
>
> We welcome you if you're having problems or you're down in the dumps of if you don't like "organized religion." . . .
>
> If you blew all your offering money partying, you're welcome here.
>
> We welcome those who are inked, pierced, or both.
>
> We offer a special welcome to those who could use a prayer right now, had religion shoved down your throat as a kid or got lost in traffic and wound up here by mistake.
>
> We welcome . . . seekers and doubters.
>
> [We welcome] you![4]

Conclusion

You need to know that kind of grace is what marks this place. I can't speak for every church, but I can speak for this one. And you need it. I need it.

The world tells us to play a big game of hide-and-seek. Everybody hide, because if you come out and are found, you will be rejected. Condemned. So hiding as long as you can is how you play the game.

Jesus wants the church to be the place where a huge, collective, "olly olly oxen free" is shouted at the top of our lungs. It's time to be found. It's safe to be found, because it's time to come home and find acceptance, forgiveness, truth, and grace.

Don't you want that? Well, around here, we do. It has marked us from day one. In fact, let me tell you a story that I got permission to tell.

A young woman and her roommate attended college here in Charlotte. These girls were the epitome of party girls, and one of them got pregnant.

It rocked their world; they didn't know what to do. So they talked about it and said, "Why don't we try going to a church?" So they randomly picked a church near campus (the University of North Carolina at Charlotte).

They attended that church for a few weeks. About the third week, the story finally came out that one of the girls was pregnant. Shortly after, they received a visit from the pastor, who told them, "You're not welcome here. You're not our type."

The two young women walked away heartbroken. They were left thinking that God was not the answer, and God's people clearly were not the answer.

A couple of weeks later they got a flyer in the mail about a new church that was starting up called Mecklenburg Community Church. The flyer invited them to its very first service on October 4, 1992.

They decided to give it one last shot, and they came to Meck that first service we ever held—back when we met in the Hilton hotel. And within six weeks both of them had given their lives to Christ, and I baptized those two women.

Later, the girl who had been pregnant moved away, but the other one stayed on. Later she was introduced to a wonderful, godly man, a friend of mine. And I had the pleasure of officiating at their wedding.

Eventually I had the privilege to dedicate her three children and then later had the joy of baptizing each of them.

This young woman ended up joining our staff and becoming one of our senior leaders. She has been with me the whole time—this entire twenty-year run. And I can't imagine what my life would have been like without her. She has babysat my children, and I love her as a daughter.

She was almost lost—all because of judgmentalism. She was almost lost because of everything Jesus is *not* about.

So why do I tell you all that? Because we are imperfect. There's all kinds of stuff around here that people are dealing with. Beginning with their pastor.

But we're going to love each other—and we do love each other. There is radical grace and acceptance here. You can come here with your junk and with your questions and explore what God has for your life.

You will not be condemned. You will be challenged, but you will be accepted and loved.

And who knows, maybe one day I'll have the privilege of baptizing you, or even your children. How cool would that be?

Okay, let's stand for a closing prayer.

Appendix B

The Spirituality Grid

The following is the transcription of a talk delivered at Mecklenburg Community Church in 2013 titled "The Spirituality Grid." It was the final installment of a series titled "Ultimate Life Coaching." The intent was to address the "spiritual, but not religious" mindset of our day. It used a large axis prop on stage—illustrated below—that was filled in as the talk went on. As the final talk of the series, it also ended with a challenge to fully surrender to Christ.

◻ ◻ ◻

Introduction

For the last few weeks we've been on a life-coaching journey. We've called it "ultimate" because it's been a look at the kind of coaching the Bible brings on our life, on ultimate issues.

It has not been just tips and techniques about better workouts or financial planning. It has been life principles about the importance of waiting on God's activity, instead of just our own; doing what we are made to do in terms of gifts, passions, and personality type; and finding and following the will of God through Scripture, prayer, circumstances, and counsel.

Today as we bring the series to an end, we're going to look at the most important life-coaching principle of all. It's the most important because it's about optimally integrating your life at its deepest level. So let's jump in.

When it comes to the deepest part of who you are, there are two dynamics at play. One has to do with spirituality, and the other has to do with religion. Let me explain both ideas.

Spirituality has to do with what you're open to, sensitive toward, in your inner world. If you ask someone, "Would you consider yourself spiritual?" most would say yes. Because they believe in God, they pray, and they consider that part of their inner world important—so they want it open to being alive and real.

Then there's *religion*, which has to do with how you have aligned your spirituality. That means how you have brought your spirituality into alignment with a set of beliefs, a particular faith tradition, a set of Scriptures revealed by a God.

Now, I know both of these have their warped definitions. You can define *spirituality* as being all gooey-eyed and sentimental, with "Praise the Lord this" and "Praise the Lord that" coming out of someone's mouth. And you reject it.

You can define *religion* as everything organized and corrupt, legalistic and lifeless and dead. And you reject it.

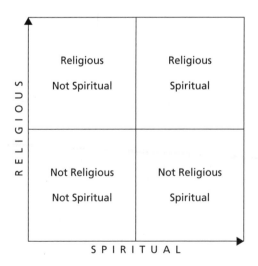

But make no mistake—where you stand with religion and spirituality, at their best and purest and most authentic and real, is the key to organizing your inner world. So let's see how to best do that, and we'll use a vertical and horizontal axis to explain it and then look at the four places we can find ourselves.

Not Spiritual, Not Religious

First, your life may be not spiritual and not religious. If you're in this category, you most likely call yourself an atheist. You don't believe in God or anything else that is transcendent or supernatural. You don't pray because you don't believe there's anyone, or anything, to pray to.

Not many people fall into this category. According to recent studies, at best only 6 percent of the entire U.S. population call themselves an atheist. Some studies show it as low as 3 percent.

That means that most of us—as high as 97 percent of us—fall into one of the other three categories. And for good reason. Not religious and not spiritual does not have much of an inner world, much less a place of hope or promise. Even those who put themselves there know that in the end it leads to despair.

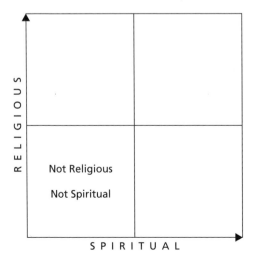

It was Friedrich Nietzsche who famously said, "God is dead." But in that famous essay, his next words are the most haunting: "We have killed him. . . . How shall we comfort ourselves, the murderers of all murderers?"[1]

Religious, Not Spiritual

The next category is when you are religious, but not spiritual. This is when you have all the form and function, rules and ritual, dogma and doctrine, but not much else. At its worst, this is just being a Pharisee, a hypocrite.

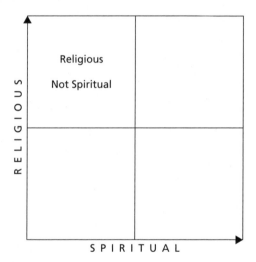

Jesus had little regard for those in this category. This is his assessment of their position:

> What sorrow awaits you teachers of religious law and you Pharisees. Hypocrites! For you are so careful to clean the outside of the cup and the dish, but inside you are filthy—full of greed and self-indulgence! You blind Pharisee! First wash the inside of the cup and the dish, and then the outside will become clean, too.
>
> What sorrow awaits you teachers of religious law and you Pharisees. Hypocrites! For you are like whitewashed tombs—beautiful on the

outside but filled on the inside with dead people's bones and all sorts of impurity. Outwardly you look like righteous people, but inwardly your hearts are filled with hypocrisy and lawlessness. (Matt. 23:25–28 NLT)

And most of us would cheer Jesus on with those words, wouldn't we? We hate religious hypocrisy. People who say one thing and do another; people who pose and posture as being spiritual, when they aren't. It's one of the reasons we hate anything related to religion.

Yet many people are in this category and don't know it. They may not be Pharisees or hypocrites, but they have *churchianity*, not Christianity. They have religion but not relationship. They go by law but seldom by grace. They are members; their name is on the roll. They attend. They subscribe. But it doesn't mean anything. It makes them feel good about themselves, but they aren't any different than anybody else.

It's dead. Lifeless. Meaningless. Ritual and form. And that's how it's played out in their life. You ask them about Christianity or faith and they say, "I'm Catholic," or "I'm Baptist." But you didn't ask them about religion—you asked about relationship.

Jesus talked about those kinds of people too: "These people honor me with their lips, but their hearts are far from me. Their worship is a farce" (Matt. 15:8–9 NLT).

And he also said,

Not everyone who calls out to me, "Lord! Lord!" will enter the Kingdom of Heaven. Only those who actually do the will of my Father in heaven will enter. On judgment day many will say to me, "Lord! Lord! We prophesied in your name and cast out demons in your name and performed many miracles in your name." But I will reply, "I never knew you." (Matt. 7:21–23 NLT)

Or as Eugene Peterson paraphrases those verses,

Knowing the correct password—saying "Master, Master," for instance—isn't going to get you anywhere with me. What is required is serious obedience—*doing* what my Father wills. I can see it now—at the Final Judgment thousands strutting up to me and saying, "Master, we preached the Message, we bashed the demons, our God-sponsored projects had everyone talking." And do you know what I am going to say? "You missed the boat. All you did was use me to make yourselves important. You don't impress me one bit." (Matt. 7:21–23 Message)

Spiritual, Not Religious

Next is by far the most popular category: being spiritual but not religious. For a lot of people, this is to avoid hypocrisy, to avoid wearing the Christian label, to avoid seeming to be something you're not—but still holding on to God.

In fact, this is the fastest-growing religious demographic in the nation. It's been called the rise of the *nones*. That's n-o-n-e-s, not n-u-n-s.

When asked about religion, they didn't answer "Baptist" or "Catholic" or any other defined faith. They said, "I don't want to say I'm any religion."

Between 1990 and 2008, the number of *nones* nearly doubled in size, from 8 percent to over 15 percent. Then between 2008 and 2012—just four years—it went from 15 percent to 20 percent. That's one out of every five people. And for people under thirty, it makes up one out of every three.

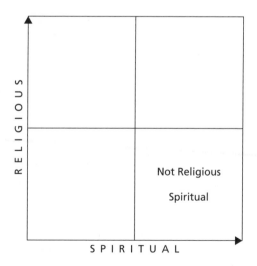

The *nones* now make up the nation's fastest-growing religious category. If you're spiritual, but not religious,

> you're not an atheist,
> you still believe in God,
> you still whisper a prayer every now and then,
> you're spiritual—or at least open to spirituality,
> you just don't want to be tied to anything specific.

When it comes to content, dogma, orthodoxy—anything spelled out or offering a system of beliefs or membership—that's what you've rejected. When pressed as to what you hold to, you say, "Nothing in particular." You don't want the label.

I recently read an interview with Marcus Mumford, the twenty-six-year-old lead singer of the phenomenally successful British band Mumford & Sons. One of my favorite bands, actually. Mumford is the son of John and Eleanor Mumford, the national leaders of Vineyard Church in the U.K. and Ireland, part of the international, evangelical Christian Vineyard Movement. He recently married actress Carey Mulligan, whom he'd met years earlier at a Christian youth camp.

Marcus is the main lyricist for the band, and their music is filled with the themes and imagery of faith—often drawing specifically on the Christian tradition. They "explore relationships with God and others; fears and doubts; sin, redemption, and most of all, grace."[2]

In a *Rolling Stone* interview, however, the reporter asked him whether he "still consider[s] himself a Christian."

This is his answer:

> I don't really like that word. It comes with so much baggage. So, no, I wouldn't call myself a Christian. I think the word just conjures up all these religious images that I don't really like. I have my personal views about the person of Jesus and who he was . . . [but] I've kind of separated myself from the culture of Christianity.[3]

While describing his spiritual journey as a "work in progress," Mumford said that he's never doubted the existence of God. Is that how you feel? If so, you're not alone; it's how a lot of people feel.

Many of us have rejected what's wrong with religion. I have. I tell people all the time that Christianity isn't about religion; it's about a relationship. And it's true. It is. But when I say that, I'm talking about the warped definition of religion. Not the real definition of religion. Because Christianity isn't just about being spiritual. It's about realities. It has content, substance, and specificity. There isn't just a vocabulary that goes with it, but a dictionary. It's about truth.

It's fine to pray, but who, or what, are you praying to? Are you praying to a rock, a tree, a spirit, an angel, a god? It matters. If you're praying to the one and only true God, who is that God? And if you like Jesus, well then who he is matters. If Jesus claimed to be that God in human form, come to planet Earth to show the way, where do you stand with that Jesus?

You can't just "like" Jesus on Facebook. You can't just follow him on Twitter, picking and choosing what you "favorite" or want to retweet. Either he was who he said he was, or he wasn't. I mean, listen to what he said about himself: "I am the way, the truth, and the life" (John 14:6 NLT). Not *a* way, or *a* truth, or *a* life, but *the*!

As C. S. Lewis once wrote, you can write Jesus off as a lunatic or as the greatest con man in all of history, or you can fall down at his feet in worship. But you can't just say he was a decent guy who occasionally said some things you like. He's either Lord, a lunatic, or a liar. Liars and lunatics aren't to be followed. Lords are meant to be worshiped.

Spirituality is not simply a feeling or a set of practices or a disposition. It's either rooted in reality or it's not. It's like climbing up a rope—it matters what the rope is tied to. And it needs to be tied to something.

I know, I know—the big idea that we keep hearing is that there are lots of roads to God. There isn't just one truth. There isn't just one religion.

The idea is that searching for God is like climbing a mountain. Since everyone knows that there is not just *one* way to climb a mountain—mountains are too big for that—there must be any number of paths that can be taken. So we tend to look at all of the ideas about God throughout all the religions of the world as just different ways up the mountain, because God is too big to be thought of or worshiped in just one way.

Therefore all of the names of God in all of the world's religions all name the same God. Jesus had one word in response: No.

That doesn't mean there can't be some good in other religions. There is nothing in the teaching of Jesus that says that to believe in the truth of Christianity you have to believe that every other world religion is completely wrong all the way through. You don't have to deny the existence of some truth or goodness in other perspectives.

Think of it in terms of arithmetic. There is one and only one right answer to "two plus two"—and that's four. But if you answered "6," it would be a lot closer than answering "37." While there is only one right answer, some answers are closer to being right than others.

But that doesn't mean that all religions are basically the same, or offer the same path to God, or are on equal footing, or will land me in a right relationship with the living God. Even the Dalai Lama has said that the central doctrines of Buddhism and Christianity are not compatible. He has said himself that you cannot be a Buddhist Christian or a Christian Buddhist.

He is right. Christianity believes in a personal God; Buddhism does not even believe in a Higher Being. Buddhism is, essentially, an atheistic religion.

That's kind of a divide, don't you think? That's not the two different ways up the same mountain—those are different mountains. And that's the way it works across the board.

Christians believe there is one God; Hindus believe there are millions.

Christians embrace Jesus as God himself in human form; Muslims don't even rank him at the top of the prophets, much less the Savior of the world.

Now, whenever you have divisions like that, you only have two options: (1) you can say that somebody is right in that particular area and everybody else is wrong, or (2) you can say that everyone is wrong in that area. But what you can't say is that everybody believes about the same thing. That would be intellectually dishonest. Unless God is a senile, confused, muddled, schizophrenic, unbalanced being who isn't sure what he stands for, then there *is* religious truth and religious falsehood.

The areas of disagreement are not trivial in nature. They deal with the very nature of God, the identity of Jesus, and how we enter into a relationship with God. So while being spiritual but not religious sounds good, when you really understand what *religion* is about at its best and most authentic and most clear, you will see that it's not good. It's deceptive. It means you believe in little more than yourself—that there's no truth outside of you. And it's your own little spirituality and your own little belief system, and what you've done is made yourself your own little god.

Spiritual and Religious

That brings us to our final category: spiritual and religious. This is when you get everything aligned: The head and the heart. Belief in God and belief in his Word. You pray, but you also listen. You know, and you do. You believe, and you live.

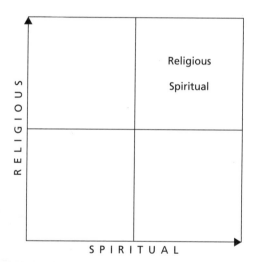

Jesus talks about this perfect integration in one of his most famous word pictures:

> So why do you keep calling me "Lord, Lord!" when you don't do what I say? I will show you what it's like when someone comes to me, listens to my teaching, and then follows it. It is like a person building a house who

digs deep and lays the foundation on solid rock. When the floodwaters
rise and break against that house, it stands firm because it is well built.
But anyone who hears and doesn't obey is like a person who builds
a house without a foundation. When the floods sweep down against
that house, it will collapse into a heap of ruins. (Luke 6:46–49 NLT)

See how this works?

Conclusion

Now, let me tell you about my grid. I've been in every one of these
categories. I started out in the not spiritual, not religious category. In
fact, I drifted in and out of this one a lot in my early years.

My family of origin was, to say the least, inconsistent with church
involvement. In fact, I don't recall going to church at all during my
high school years.

So there wasn't much in terms of religion, even in the worst sense
of the word, much less the best. And I wasn't walking with Jesus at
all. I mean, I had some beliefs, but they didn't matter. I did what I
wanted to do. That, I can tell you, wasn't very Jesusy.

But then I developed a sense of religion—but the Pharisee, hypocritical kind. Meaning I began filling my head with knowledge, but my
heart was far from God. I was always drawn to rational, intellectual,
scientific kind of stuff. Theology to me was a mental game. An exer-
cise. A chess match. And I was good at it. And like a lot of people, I
was well-read, smart. And I liked boxing matches with people who I
thought weren't quite up to par. I at least wanted to see if I could win.

I remember when I went to college, my freshman roommate was a
Mormon. In terms of a theological debate, he was low-hanging fruit.
So one night after more than a few beers, I started slicing and dicing
the Book of Mormon and Mormonism: the lack of an archaeological
record for their claims, the ridiculous theology, their special under-
wear, and so on.

It was slick. And to be honest, it was true. He was lost, scrambling,
outmatched. But then he said one thing that ended the conversation.
He said, "Jim, how can you say anything at all to me with the way
you live?"

There was nothing I could say. He was right. Christianity may have been true and right, but I wasn't. All I had done was go from no religion, no spirituality, to the worst of religion without spirituality.

Well, then my life went into a serious tailspin. The details aren't important, but I hit rock bottom in every conceivable way to the point that even I could see it.

I recall one night in particular—my life came into focus. This wasn't who I wanted to be. This wasn't the path I wanted to be on. For the first time in my life, I saw my trajectory. And it wasn't a good one.

I had been living in a bubble of believing that how I was living didn't matter or was no big deal. That bubble burst. I saw myself for who I was: lost, broken, empty.

And then I got spiritual. I dropped the pretense of religion and started hungering for God. Thinking about God. Praying to God.

But even that didn't take me very far because I still wasn't connected to living for him. Obeying him. Submitting to him. I was spiritual, but not religious—and I mean religious in the best sense of the word. It didn't translate into something with muscle, strength, content, specificity. It wasn't tied to Jesus—what he said, what he did. No obedience, no leadership.

A few months later some friends invited me to a campus gathering sponsored by a Christian ministry to college students. They had asked me a dozen times before, and I always blew it off. Not now. They asked; I went.

The speaker gave a talk about a simple idea: Jesus as Savior *and* Lord. Forgiver *and* Leader. Real religion and authentic spirituality—combined. I'll never forget what part of the teaching of Jesus he read from:

> Large crowds were traveling with Jesus, and turning to them he said: "If anyone comes to me and does not hate his father and mother, wife and children, brothers and sisters—yes, even their own life—such a person cannot be my disciple. And whoever does not carry their cross and follow me cannot be my disciple.
>
> Suppose one of you wants to build a tower. Won't you first sit down and estimate the cost to see if you have enough money to complete it? For if you lay the foundation and are not able to finish it, everyone

who sees it will ridicule you, saying, "This person began to build and wasn't able to finish."

Or suppose a king is about to go to war against another king. Won't he first sit down and consider whether he is able with ten thousand men to oppose the one coming against him with twenty thousand? If he is not able, he will send a delegation while the other is still a long way off and will ask for terms of peace. In the same way, those of you who do not give up everything you have cannot be my disciples.

Salt is good, but if it loses its saltiness, how can it be made salty again? It is fit neither for the soil nor for the manure pile; it is thrown out.

Whoever has ears to hear, let them hear. (Luke 14:25–35)

On that day, my ears heard. On that night, I became a Christian— a real one.

I remember talking to the person who brought me, and I kept saying, over and over again, "But so much will have to change . . . so much will have to change."

I really got the fullness of it, the completeness of it. This was going to have to be a complete surrender. This wasn't a game. This was about my life—on this earth and in the life to come after my life on earth was over.

It was about commitment. Real commitment. It was about finally surrendering everything I had, everything I was, to Christ. It was about giving up being religious without being spiritual, and spiritual without being religious. It was about going all the way. It was about embracing all of what Jesus meant for my life. As *the* way, *the* truth, and *the* life.

Where are you? More importantly, where do you want to be? Do you know why you're here today, listening to this? It's because you are being called, today, by Jesus, to make a decision about your life.

I'm not calling you; he is. And it's not about raising your hand. It's not about walking down an aisle. It's not about checking a box on a card. It's not even about mouthing a prayer that you may have mouthed a dozen times before. It's about surrendering your life—all of it.

There's only one of these four boxes your life can be in that will give you the life you long for, the life you're called to, the life that *is* life. Only one.

You don't need me to tie this with a bow and end in some trite, contrived, manufactured way. You don't need me to lead you in a prayer or get you to *do* anything. You're an adult. If you need to pray, you know what you need to pray. If you need to decide, you know what you need to decide.

My role is simple: to challenge you to do it—like someone challenged me.

So leave whenever you're ready and you want to. But don't leave before you've decided who you want to be and how you want to live—and have told God.

Notes

Chapter 1 The Rise of the *Nones*

1. Joshua E. Keating, "Megatrends That Weren't," *Foreign Policy*, September/October 2011: 92, http://www.foreignpolicy.com/articles/2011/08/15/megatrends_that_werent.

2. ARIS, "American Nones: The Profile of the No Religion Population," Trinity College, http://commons.trincoll.edu/aris/files/2011/08/NONES_08.pdf.

3. Cathy Lee Grossman, "Almost All Denominations Losing Ground: Faith Is Shifting, Drifting or Vanishing Outright," *USA Today*, March 9, 2009, 1A, 6A.

4. Rachel Zoll, "Survey: We're Losing Our Religion," Associated Press, March 9, 2009, in the *Charlotte Observer*, March 9, 2009, 5A.

5. "America Becoming Less Christian, Survey Finds," CNN.com, posted March 12, 2009, http://www.cnn.com/2009/LIVING/wayoflife/03/09/us.religion.less.christian/index.html.

6. Lance Dickie, "US Religion ID Inching to 'None,'" *Seattle Times*, printed in the *Charlotte Observer*, March 24, 2009, 11A.

7. Adelle M. Banks, "None of Thee Above," Religion News Service, in the *Charlotte Observer*, March 14, 2009, 1E and 3E.

8. ARIS, "American Nones."

9. For the latest report, see Barry A. Kosmin and Juhem Navarro-River, "The Transformation of Generation X: Shifts in Religious and Political Self-Identification, 1990–2008," http://commons.trincoll.edu/aris/files/2012/05/ARISGENX2012.pdf.

10. Michelle Boorstein, "Huge Religion Survey: Gen X-ers Less Christian, Less Republican," *Washington Post*, May 31, 2012, http://www.washingtonpost.com/blogs/under-god/post/huge-religion-survey-gen-x-ers-less-christian-less-republican/2012/05/31/gJQAcjpA5U_blog.html.

11. Christian Smith and Melina Lundquist Denton, *Soul Searching: The Religious and Spiritual Lives of American Teenagers* (New York: Oxford University Press, 2005);

Christian Smith with Patricia Snell, *Souls in Transition: The Religious and Spiritual Lives of Emerging Adults* (New York: Oxford University Press, 2009).

12. Smith and Snell, *Souls in Transition*, 145.

13. Ibid., 168.

14. Pew Forum on Religion and Public Life, "Nones on the Rise," http://www.pewforum.org/Unaffiliated/nones-on-the-rise.aspx. Leading articles on the release of the survey include: Cathy Lynn Grossman, "As Protestants Decline, Those with No Religion Gain," *USA Today*, October 9, 2012, 1A, http://www.usatoday.com/story/news/nation/2012/10/08/nones-protestant-religion-pew/1618445/; Michelle Boorstein, "One in Five Americans Reports No Religious Affiliation, Study Says," *Washington Post*, October 9, 2012, http://www.washingtonpost.com/local/one-in-five-americans-reports-no-religious-affiliation-study-says/2012/10/08/a7599664-11c8-11e2-855a-c9ee6c045478_story.html?hpid=z1; "Protestants No Longer the Majority in US, Study Says," Fox News, http://www.foxnews.com/us/2012/10/09/protestants-no-longer-majority-in-us-study-says/?test=latestnews#ixzz28nCef15G; Laurie Goodstein, "Number of Protestant Americans Is in Steep Decline, Study Finds," *New York Times*, October 9, 2012, http://www.nytimes.com/2012/10/10/us/study-finds-that-the-number-of-protestant-americans-is-declining.html?hp; Teresa Watanabe, "Protestants No Longer a Majority of Americans, Study Finds," *Los Angeles Times*, October 9, 2012, http://www.latimes.com/news/local/la-me-protestants-20121010,0,70131.story.

15. Steven Swinford, "Number of Christians in England and Wales Falls by More than 4 million," *Telegraph*, December 11, 2012, http://www.telegraph.co.uk/news/religion/9736609/Number-of-Christians-in-England-and-Wales-falls-by-more-than-4-million.html.

16. Katherine Bindley, "Religion among Americans Hits Low Point, As More People Say They Have No Religious Affiliation: Report," *Huffington Post*, March 1, 2012, http://www.huffingtonpost.com/2013/03/13/religion-america-decline-low-no-affiliation-report_n_2867626.html; see also Yasmin Anwar, "Americans and Religion Increasingly Parting Ways, New Survey Shows," UC Berkeley News Center, March 12, 2013, http://newscenter.berkeley.edu/2013/03/12/non-believers/.

17. Bindley, "Religion among Americans Hits Low Point"; see also Anwar, "Americans and Religion Increasingly Parting Ways."

18. These statements from Smith, Newport, Wilcox, and Kinnaman are quoted in Ruth Moon, compiler, "Is Concern Over the Rise of the 'Nones' Overblown?" *Christianity Today*, April 8, 2013, http://www.christianitytoday.com/ct/2013/april/is-concern-over-rise-of-nones-overblown.html?utm_source=ctdirect-html&utm_medium=Newsletter&utm_term=9470253&utm_content=167052631&utm_campaign=2013.

19. Dan Gilgoff, "My Take: 5 Things I Learned Editing the Belief Blog," CNN, December 31, 2012, http://religion.blogs.cnn.com/2012/12/31/my-take-5-things-i-learned-editing-the-belief-blog/.

20. "Global Data Upend Usual Picture of Christianity Trends," Anglican Communion News Service, March 19, 2013, http://www.anglicancommunion.org/acns/news.cfm/2013/3/19/ACNS5358.

21. Cathy Lynn Grossman, "Meet the 'Nones': An Emerging Force," *USA Today*, October 9, 2012, 3A, http://www.usatoday.com/story/news/nation/2012/10/09/nones-religion-pew-study/1618607/.

Chapter 2 Snapshots

1. Pew Forum, "Nones on the Rise"; Lauren Markoe, "Meet John Q. Nones: A Profile of the Fast-Growing Religiously Unaffiliated," *Religion News Service*, October 9, 2012, http://www.religionnews.com/faith/beliefs/meet-john-q-nones-a-profile-of-the-fast-growing-religiously-unaffiliated, used by permission.

2. Cathleen Falsani, "The Trouble with Labels," *Orange County Register*, April 3, 2013, Religion News Service, http://www.religionnews.com/2013/04/03/the-trouble-with-labels/.

3. Brian Hiatt, "Marcus Mumford: 'I Wouldn't Call Myself a Christian,'" *Rolling Stone*, March 13, 2013, http://www.rollingstone.com/music/news/marcus-mumford-i-wouldnt-call-myself-a-christian-20130313.

4. Falsani, "The Trouble with Labels."

5. Quoted in ibid.

6. Ibid.

7. Grossman, "As Protestants Decline."

8. Dan Merica, "Survey: One in Five Americans Has No Religion," CNN, October 9, 2012, http://religion.blogs.cnn.com/2012/10/09/survey-one-in-five-americans-is-religiously-unaffiliated/.

9. ARIS, "American Nones."

10. Cathy Lynn Grossman, "'Nones' Now 15% of Population," *USA Today*, March 9, 2009, http://usatoday30.usatoday.com/news/religion/2009-03-09-aris-survey-nones_N.htm.

11. Pew Forum, "Nones on the Rise."

12. Jonathan Rauch, "Let It Be," *Atlantic Monthly*, May 2003, 34.

13. Cathy Lynn Grossman, "For Many, 'Losing My Religion' Isn't Just a Song: It's Life," *USA Today*, January 3, 2012, http://usatoday30.usatoday.com/news/religion/story/2011-12-25/religion-god-atheism-so-what/52195274/1.

14. Phil Zuckerman, *Society without God: What the Least Religious Nations Can Tell Us about Contentment* (New York: New York University Press, 2008), 102.

15. Ibid., 109.

16. On this, see Huston Smith, *Why Religion Matters: The Fate of the Human Spirit in an Age of Disbelief* (New York: HarperSanFrancisco, 2001), 103.

Chapter 3 Lawyers, Guns, and Money

1. Sebastian Junger, *The Perfect Storm: A True Story of Men Against the Sea* (New York: W. W. Norton, 1997).

2. For more on this, see James Emery White, *Embracing the Mysterious God* (Downers Grove, IL: InterVarsity, 2003).

3. On the tenability of the theory of evolution, see Michael Behe, *Darwin's Black Box: The Biochemical Challenge to Evolution* (New York: Free Press, 1996); Phillip E. Johnson, *Darwin on Trial* (Downer's Grove, IL: Intervarsity Press, 2010); William A. Dembski, *Intelligent Design: The Bridge between Science and Technology* (Downer's Grove, IL: InterVarsity Press, 1999).

4. Robert Putnam, quoted in Heidi Glenn, "Losing Our Religion: The Growth of the 'Nones,'" National Public Radio, January 13, 2013, http://www.npr.org/blogs/thetwo-way/2013/01/14/169164840/losing-our-religion-the-growth-of-the-nones.

5. Warren Zevon, "Lawyers, Guns and Money," *Excitable Boy* (Asylum, 1978).

6. Charles E. Shepard, *Forgiven: The Rise and Fall of Jim Bakker and the PTL Ministry* (New York: Atlantic Monthly Press, 1989), 275–80.

7. Pew Forum, "Nones on the Rise."

8. Bindley, "Religion among Americans Hits Low Point"; see also Anwar, "Americans and Religion Increasingly Parting Ways." See also Michael Hout and Claude S. Fischer, "Why More Americans Have No Religious Preference: Politics and Generations," *American Sociological Review* 67, no. 2 (April, 2002): 165–90.

9. James Davison Hunter, *To Change the World* (Oxford: Oxford University Press, 2010), 107.

10. James Emery White, *Christ Among the Dragons* (Downers Grove, IL: Inter-Varsity, 2010).

11. John Winthrop, *A Modell of Christian Charity* (1630), cited in Conrad Cherry, *God's New Israel: Religious Interpretations of American Destiny* (Englewood Cliffs, NJ: Prentice-Hall, Inc., 1971), 43.

12. Cherry, *God's New Israel*, vii.

13. Mark A. Noll, Nathan O. Hatch, and George M. Marsden, *The Search for Christian America*, expanded edition (Colorado Springs: Helmers and Howard, 1989).

14. Dan Savage, "What God Wants," *New York Times Book Review*, April 14, 2013, 1, http://www.nytimes.com/2013/04/14/books/review/does-jesus-really-love-me-by-jeff-chu.html?pagewanted=all. The Minchin video can be found at http://www.youtube.com/watch?v=r0xQcEH7Dqo.

15. David Kinnaman and Gabe Lyons, *Unchristian: What a New Generation Really Thinks about Christianity* (Grand Rapids, MI: Baker, 2007); research from the Barna Group. See also, David Van Biema, "Christianity's Image Problem," Time.com, October 2, 2007, http://jp.youtube.com/watch?v=ZlFqhHJczDs.

Chapter 4 A Post-Christian World

1. David McCullough, *John Adams* (New York: Simon & Schuster, 2001), 647.

2. On the history of the idea of America as a chosen nation, see Cherry, *God's New Israel*.

3. Mitchell Landsberg, "Evangelical Leaders Echo Obama, Say US Not a Christian Nation," *Los Angeles Times*, July 31, 2012, http://www.latimes.com/news/politics/la-pn-evangelical-leaders-echo-obama-say-us-not-a-christian-nation-20120731,0,838080.story; "United States: Christian Nation or Mission Field?" National Association of Evangelicals, news release, http://www.nae.net/resources/news/793-united-states-christian-nation-or-mission-field.

4. Jeremy Weber, "15 Measurements of Whether Americans Are Post-Christian," *Christianity Today*, posted April 15, 2013, http://blog.christianitytoday.com/ctliveblog/archives/2013/04/barna-measures-nones-post-christian-americans.html?utm_source=feedburner&utm_medium=feed&utm_campaign=Feed%3A+christianitytoday%2Fctliveblog+%28Christianity+Today+Liveblog%29&utm_content=Google+Reader. For the actual Barna report, "How Post-Christian Is U.S. Society?" see http://www.barna.org/culture-articles/613-how-post-christian-is-us-society.

5. Pew Forum, "Nones on the Rise."

6. Ibid.

7. Peter Berger, *The Sacred Canopy: Elements of a Sociological Theory of Religion* (Garden City, NY: Anchor/Doubleday, 1969). An excellent analysis can also be

found in Robert Wuthnow, *The Struggle for America's Soul: Evangelicals, Liberals, and Secularism* (Grand Rapids, MI: Eerdmans, 1989).

8. This discussion was first presented, and is here adapted from, my earlier book, *Serious Times* (Downers Grove, IL: InterVarsity, 2006).

9. Berger, *Sacred Canopy*, 107. See also David Martin, *A General Theory of Secularization* (Oxford: Blackwell, 1978), and Martin E. Marty, *The Modern Schism* (London: SCM, 1969).

10. Richard John Neuhaus, *The Naked Public Square: Religion and Democracy in America* (Grand Rapids, MI: Eerdmans, 1984).

11. On this, see Martin E. Marty, *A Short History of Christianity*, 2nd ed. (Philadelphia: Fortress, 1987), 222–23.

12. E. F. Schumaker, *A Guide for the Perplexed* (New York: Harper Perennial, 1977), 1–2.

13. Smith, *Why Religion Matters*, 193–94.

14. C. S. Lewis, *The Weight of Glory and Other Addresses*, rev. and exp. ed. (New York: Collier/Macmillan, 1980), 7.

15. For an introduction to the debate, see William H. Swatos Jr. and Daniel V. A. Olson, eds., *The Secularization Debate* (Lanham, MD: Rowman and Littlefield, 2000), for the Association for the Sociology of Religion.

16. Christian Smith, "Introduction: Rethinking the Secularization of American Public Life," in *The Secular Revolution*, ed. Christian Smith (Berkeley: University of California Press, 2003), 5.

17. Peter L. Berger, ed., *The Desecularization of the World: Resurgent Religion and World Politics* (Washington, DC: Ethics and Public Policy Center/Grand Rapids, MI: Eerdmans, 1999), 2.

18. Ibid., 10.

19. Steve Bruce, *God Is Dead: Secularization in the West* (Oxford: Blackwell, 2002), 147.

20. Ray Kroc, *Grinding It Out: The Making of McDonald's* (Chicago: Contemporary Books, 1977), 124.

21. Os Guinness, *The Gravedigger File: Papers on the Subversion of the Modern Church* (Downers Grove, IL: InterVarsity, 1983), 74; cf. Thomas Luckmann, *The Invisible Religion* (New York: Macmillan, 1967). Perhaps the best investigation into this dynamic of modernity is offered by Robert Bellah, Richard Madsen, William M. Sullivan, and Ann Swidler, *Habits of the Heart: Individualism and Commitment in American Life* (San Francisco: Harper and Row, 1985). A chronicle of America's privatization of faith can be found in Phillip L. Berman, *The Search for Meaning: Americans Talk About What They Believe and Why* (New York: Ballantine, 1990).

22. Noted by John Naisbitt and Patricia Aburdene, *Megatrends 2000: Ten New Directions for the 1990's* (New York: William Morrow, 1990); for contemporary society see in particular, "Spirituality, Yes. Organized Religion, No," in *Megatrends 2000*, 275. A similar point is made by George Barna, *The Frog in the Kettle* (Ventura, CA: Regal, 1990), 41–42, 117.

23. Theodore Roszak, *Where the Wasteland Ends* (Garden City, NY: Anchor, 1973), 412.

24. Page Smith, *Killing the Spirit: Higher Education in America* (New York: Viking, 1990), 5.

25. Berger, *Sacred Canopy*, 127. The historical background to this stream of modernity is charted in Nathan O. Hatch, *The Democratization of American Christianity* (New Haven, CT: Yale, 1989).

26. Guinness, *Gravedigger File*, 93.

27. Ibid., 94. The idea of religion as a canopy serves as the motif for Martin E. Marty's exploration of modern American religion, *The Irony of It All, 1893–1919*, vol. 1, *Modern American Religion* (Chicago: University of Chicago Press, 1986).

28. See Samuel Eliot Morison, Henry Steele Commanger, and William E. Leuchtenburg, *The Growth of the American Republic*, 7th ed. (New York: Oxford University Press, 1980), vol. 2, 108, note 3, cited by Louis Menand, *The Metaphysical Club: A Story of Ideas in America* (New York: Farrar, Straus and Giroux, 2001), 381.

29. For one of the most thorough and insightful treatments of issues related to this in regard to Christian thought and enterprise, see Harold Netland, *Encountering Religious Pluralism: The Challenge to Christian Faith and Mission* (Downers Grove, IL: InterVarsity, 2001).

30. Langdon Gilkey, *Through the Tempest: Theological Voyages in a Pluralistic Culture* (Minneapolis: Fortress, 1991), 21.

31. Harold O. J. Brown, "Evangelicals and Social Ethics," in *Evangelical Affirmations,* ed. Kenneth S. Kantzer and Carl F. H. Henry (Grand Rapids, MI: Academie/Zondervan, 1990), 279.

32. Harold A. Netland, *Dissonant Voices: Religious Pluralism and the Question of Truth* (Grand Rapids, MI: Eerdmans, 1991), 30.

33. Allan Bloom, *The Closing of the American Mind* (New York: Simon and Schuster, 1987), 26.

34. James Turner, *Without God, Without Creed: The Origins of Unbelief in America* (Baltimore: Johns Hopkins Press, 1985), xii, 266–67.

35. Grossman, "Almost All Denominations Losing Ground"; Zoll, "Survey"; "America Becoming Less Christian, Survey Finds." See also Dickie, "U.S. Religion ID Inching to 'None'"; Banks, "None of Thee Above."

36. "64% Believe Jesus Christ Rose from the Dead," Rasmussen Reports, March 29, 2013, http://www.rasmussenreports.com/public_content/lifestyle/holidays/march_2013/64_believe_jesus_christ_rose_from_the_dead.

37. Uwe Siemon-Netto, "Analysis: Atheism Worldwide in Decline," United Press International, March 1, 2005, http://www.upi.com/Business_News/Security-Industry/2005/03/01/Analysis-Atheism-worldwide-in-decline/UPI-20691109700930/.

Chapter 5 Bad Religion

1. Ross Douthat, *Bad Religion: How We Became a Nation of Heretics* (New York: Free Press, 2012). See also "The Core Beliefs of America's 'Spiritual but Not Religious' Teachers," *Preaching Today*, http://www.preachingtoday.com/illustrations/2012/june/2061112.html.

2. Neale Donald Walsch quoted in Douthat, *Bad Religion*, 216.

3. Paulo Coelho quoted in ibid.

4. Elizabeth Gilbert quoted in ibid.

5. James Redfield and Paulo Coelho quoted in ibid.

6. Pew Forum, "Nones on the Rise."

7. Rabbi Marc Gellman and Monsignor Thomas Hartman, *How Do You Spell God?* (New York: Morrow Junior Books, 1995), 19–24.

8. Material in this section and in the next section on "Wikiality" also appeared in my book *Christ Among the Dragons*. See James Emery White, *Christ Among the Dragons* (Downers Grove, IL: InterVarsity Press, 2010), 24–26.

9. From the broadcast premiere of *The Colbert Report* on Comedy Central Network, October 17, 2005, http://www.colbertnation.com/the-colbert-report-videos/24039/october-17-2005/the-word—truthiness.

10. "'Truthiness' Voted 2005 Word of the Year," Associated Press, January 7, 2006, http://www.nbcnews.com/id/10745438/; "New Words of 2005," *National Public Radio Morning Edition*, December 30, 2005, audio file, http://www.npr.org/templates/story/story.php?storyId=5075545; to view *The Colbert Report* segment, http://www.comedycentral.com/sitewide/media_player/play.jhtml?itemId=24039. See also "Colbert's 'Truthiness' Strikes a Chord," *USA Today*, August 28, 2006, 1D.

11. For a direct link to Colbert's take on "wikiality," go to http://www.colbertnation.com/the-colbert-report-videos/72347/july-31-2006/the-word--wikiality.

12. Brock Read, "'Wikimania' Participants Give the Online Encyclopedia Mixed Reviews," *Chronicle of Higher Education,* September 1, 2006, A62, http://www.chronicle.com/article/Wikimania-Participants/4948.

13. Ibid.

14. Colbert, "Wikiality," http://www.colbertnation.com/the-colbert-report-videos/72347/july-31-2006/the-word---wikiality.

15. Marshall Poe, "The Hive," *Atlantic Monthly*, September 2006.

16. This illustration also appears in White, *Christ Among the Dragons*, 38–39.

17. Adam McKay and Will Ferrell, *Talladega Nights: The Ballad of Ricky Bobby*, directed by Adam McKay, Sony Pictures, 2006.

18. For example, see "Malcolm Gladwell: Guru of the Underdogs," Tina Rosenberg, *The Atlantic*, September 18, 2013, http://www.theatlantic.com/magazine/archive/2013/10/the-underdogs-guru/309458/; Christopher F. Chabris, "Book Review: *David and Goliath* by Malcolm Gladwell," *The Wall Street Journal*, September 28, 2013, http://online.wsj.com/article/SB10001424052702304713704579093090254007968.html.

19. Chabris, "*David and Goliath.*"

20. Karl Menninger, *Whatever Became of Sin?* (New York: Hawthorn Books, 1973).

21. James Tozer, "Is It a Sin? Christian Words Deleted from Oxford Dictionary," *Daily Mail*, December 7, 2008, http://www.dailymail.co.uk/news/article-1092668/Is-sin-Christian-words-deleted-Oxford-dictionary.html#.

22. Keith Ablow, "Can Sex between Brothers and Sisters Ever Be Normal?" Fox News, September 11, 2012, http://www.foxnews.com/opinion/2012/09/11/can-sex-between-brothers-and-sisters-ever-be-normal/?intcmp=features#ixzz26CRToCZN. See also "'The Notebook's Director Nick Cassavetes Says of Incest: 'Who Gives a Damn?'" Fox News, September 10, 2012, http://www.foxnews.com/entertainment/2012/09/10/notebook-director-nick-cassavetes-says-incest-who-gives-damn/?intcmp=features.

23. Christian Smith, Kari Christoffersen, Hilary Davidson, and Patricia Snell Herzog, *Lost in Transition: The Dark Side of Emerging Adulthood* (Oxford: Oxford University Press, 2011), 21, 36.

24. Ibid., 22.

25. Ibid., 30.

26. Ibid., 38.

27. Ibid., 47.

28. Ibid., 48.

29. Ibid., 51.

30. Bellah et al., *Habits of the Heart*, 221.

An Interlude

1. Marc Yoder, "Top 10 Reasons Our Kids Leave Church," posted February 8, 2013, http://marc5solas.com/2013/02/08/top-10-reasons-our-kids-leave-church/.

2. White, *Christ Among the Dragons*.

3. On this, see the ministry of www.xxxchurch.com.

4. Tony Jones, former national coordinator of Emergent Village and author of *The New Christians*, as reported by "Out of Ur," *Christianity Today*, November 26, 2008. Jones's blog can be found at http://tonyj.net/.

5. Joseph Epstein, "Celebrity Culture," *Hedgehog Review: Critical Reflections on Contemporary Culture* 7, no. 1 (Spring 2005), 14.

6. Jennifer L. Geddes, "An Interview with Richard Schickel," *Hedgehog Review: Critical Reflections on Contemporary Culture* 7, no. 1 (Spring 2005).

7. *Emergent-See Po-Motivators for Emerging Christians*, http://www.spurgeon.org/~phil/posters.htm.

Chapter 6 Making Cars

1. David A. Roozen, "A Decade of Change in American Congregations 2000–2010," Faith Communities Today, http://faithcommunitiestoday.org/sites/faithcommunities today.org/files/Decade%20of%20Change%20Final_0.pdf.

2. Ibid.

3. "Catholic Church in India Says Have More Children," Fox News, October 10, 2011, http://www.foxnews.com/world/2011/10/11/catholic-church-in-india-says-have -more-children/?test=latestnews.

4. Much of this section also appears in White, *Christ Among the Dragons*, 160–61.

5. Jean M. Twenge, *Generation Me* (New York: Free Press, 2006), 1.

6. Christopher Lasch, *The Culture of Narcissism: American Life in an Age of Diminishing Expectations* (1979; repr., New York: W. W. Norton, 1991).

7. Peter Drucker, *The 5 Most Important Questions You Will Ever Ask About Your Organization* (San Francisco: Jossey-Bass, 2008).

Chapter 7 If You Build It, They Won't Come

1. See "A Study of Adults Baptized in Southern Baptist Churches, 1993," study conducted by the Home Mission Board Research Division of the Southern Baptist Convention in conjunction with the Home Mission Board Evangelism Section, reported in *Biblical Recorder* 161, no. 15 (April 15, 1995), 12.

2. Seth Godin, "Selling to People Who Haven't Bought Yet," April 20, 2012, http://sethgodin.typepad.com/seths_blog/2012/04/selling-to-people-who-havent-bought-yet.html.

3. Ibid.

4. Adapted from Gordon Aeschliman, *Cages of Pain: Healing for Disillusioned Christians* (Dallas: Word, 1991), 24–26.

5. Darren Robell, "KO'ed by Count Chocula? Why Wheaties Cereal Is Struggling," *USA Today*, http://www.usatoday.com/money/industries/food/story/2012-04-01/cnbc-wheaties-brand-declines/53885818/1.

Chapter 8 The Importance of Cause

1. Pew Forum, "Nones on the Rise."
2. Heidi Glenn, "As Social Issues Drive Young from Church, Leaders Try to Keep Them," National Public Radio, January 18, 2013, http://www.npr.org/blogs/thetwo-way/2013/01/18/169646736/as-social-issues-drive-young-from-church-leaders-try-to-keep-them.
3. On this, see Mark Galli, "On Not Transforming the World," http://www.christianitytoday.com, posted 8/09/2007.
4. Andy Crouch, *Making Culture* (Downers Grove, IL: InterVarsity, 2008).
5. James Davison Hunter, "Transforming the Culture," *Image*, Special Issue, November 2006.
6. John Stott, *The Living Church* (Downers Grove, IL: InterVarsity, 2007), 135–38.
7. T. S. Eliot, *Christianity and Culture* (1948; repr., New York: Harcourt Brace, 1967), 75.
8. The following sections have appeared on my blog as well as in White, *Christ Among the Dragons*, 77–82.
9. Stanley J. Grenz, David Guretzki, and Cherith Fee Nordling, *Pocket Dictionary of Theological Terms* (Downers Grove, IL: InterVarsity), 56.
10. Philip Edgcumbe Hughes, "Grace," in *Evangelical Dictionary of Theology*, 2nd ed., ed. Walter Elwell (Grand Rapids, MI: Baker, 2001), 519–22.
11. Charles Colson and Nancy Pearcey, *How Now Shall We Live?* (Wheaton: Tyndale, 1999), 33.
12. For an excellent introduction to the role of art in relation to culture, see H. R. Rookmaaker, *Modern Art and the Death of a Culture* (Wheaton: Crossway Books, 1994).
13. Gene Weingarten, "Pearls Before Breakfast: Can One of the Nation's Great Musicians Cut through the Fog of a DC Rush Hour? Let's Find Out," *Washington Post*, April 8, 2007, W10, http://www.washingtonpost.com/wp-dyn/content/article/2007/04/04/AR2007040401721.html; see also "A Virtuoso Ignored," *The Week*, May 4, 2007, 52–53.

Chapter 9 Grace and Truth

1. Millard Erickson, *Christian Theology* (Grand Rapids: Baker, 1998).
2. Henry Cloud, *Changes That Heal* (Grand Rapids, MI: Zondervan, 2005), 1–28.
3. Richard Carl Hoefler, *And He Told Them a Story* (Lima, OH: C.S.S. Publishing, 1979), cited in Curtis E. Liens, *The Man with Dirty Hands* (self-published, 2000).
4. Michka Assayas, *Bono: In Conversation with Michka Assayas* (New York: Riverhead Books, 2005).
5. Dietrich Bonhoeffer, *The Cost of Discipleship* (New York: Touchstone, 1995).
6. Bob Smietana, "Unitarian Faith Growing Nationwide," *USA Today*, October 2, 2012, 3A, http://www.usatoday.com/story/news/nation/2012/10/01/unitarian-faith-growing-stronger-nationwide/1607243/.

7. J. Dudley Woodbury, Russell G. Shubin, and G. Marks, "5 Reasons Muslims Convert," *Leadership Journal*, Winter 2008, www.christianitytoday.com/le/2008/winter/9.13.html.

8. On this as well as the story of C. S. Lewis, see Philip Yancey, *What's So Amazing about Grace?* (Grand Rapids: Zondervan, 1998), 32. This illustration also appears in White, *Christ Among the Dragons*, 115.

9. For the latest report, see Kosmin and Navarro-River, "Transformation of Generation X."

10. Mark Galli, "The Troubled State of Christian Preaching," *Christianity Today*, January 21, 2013, http://www.christianitytoday.com/ct/2013/january-web-only/troubled-state-of-christian-preaching.html?paging=off.

Chapter 10 A Christian Mind

1. Harry Blamires, *The Christian Mind: How Should a Christian Think?* (Ann Arbor, MI: Servant Books, 1978), 3.

2. Mark A. Noll, *The Scandal of the Evangelical Mind* (Grand Rapids, MI: Eerdmans, 1994), 3.

3. On this, see Richard Hofstadter, *Anti-Intellectualism in American Life* (New York: Vintage, 1962), 55–80; see also Noll's interaction with Hofstadter's contention in *Scandal of the Evangelical Mind,* 11–12.

4. As noted by Robert Ellsberg, ed., *Flannery O'Connor: Spiritual Writings* (Maryknoll, NY: Orbis, 2003), 49.

5. On how worldview has been treated by a variety of thinkers, see David K. Naugle Jr., *Worldview: The History of a Concept* (Grand Rapids, MI: Eerdmans, 2002).

6. Martin Luther King Jr., *Why We Can't Wait: Letter from a Birmingham Jail* (New York: Mentor/New American Library, 1964), 82.

7. John R. W. Stott, *Your Mind Matters* (Downers Grove, IL: InterVarsity, 1972), 13.

8. Thomas Cahill, *How the Irish Saved Civilization* (New York: Doubleday, 1995), 3.

9. Ibid., 193–94.

10. Ibid.

11. See James Emery White, *A Mind for God* (Downers Grove, IL: InterVarsity, 2006).

12. Susanne M. Schafer, "Forget Bayonets: Army Busts Abs in Basic Overhaul," Associated Press, reported in *Charlotte Observer*, March 17, 2010, 16A.

13. Julia Duin, "On Seeking 'a Better God,'" *Washington Times*, August 20, 2009, http://www.washingtontimes.com/news/2009/aug/20/duin-on-seeking-a-better-god/?page=all.

14. James Kaplan, "Life after *The Da Vinci Code*," *Parade Magazine*, September 13, 2009, 4, http://www.parade.com/106060/jameskaplan/13-dan-brown-life-after-da-vinci-code/.

15. Tim Funk, "A Chat with Public Radio Host Krista Tippett," Funk on Faith, *Charlotte Observer*, March 5, 2013, http://funkonfaith.blogspot.com/2013/03/a-chat-with-public-radio-host-krista.html.

16. Tim Stanley, "Christians Need to Find Some Old-Time Zeal," *Telegraph*, January 15, 2013, http://blogs.telegraph.co.uk/news/timstanley/100198311/christians-need-to-find-some-old-time-zeal/.

17. Roger Lancelyn Green and Walter Hooper, *C. S. Lewis: An Autobiography* (Orlando: Harcourt Brace, 1974), 209.

18. C. S. Lewis, *Mere Christianity* (New York: HarperCollins, 1952), ix.

19. Alan Jacobs, *The Narnian: The Life and Imagination of C. S. Lewis* (New York: HarperSanFrancisco, 2005), 213–14.

20. Stott, *Your Mind Matters*, 13.

Chapter 11 The Importance of Unity

1. I first explored the importance of this topic in *Christ Among the Dragons*, and much of this section appears there on pages 101–2 and 120–1.

2. Deborah Tannen, *The Argument Culture* (New York: Ballantine Books, 1999).

3. Janet Kornblum, "Rudeness, Threats Make the Web a Cruel World," *USA Today*, July 31, 2007, 1A, 2A, http://usatoday30.usatoday.com/tech/webguide/internetlife /2007-07-30-cruel-web_N.htm; Noam Cohen, "Defending Wikipedia's Impolite Side," *New York Times*, Augst 20, 2007, http://www.nytimes.com/2007/08/20/technology /20link.html?_r=0.

4. Peter Wood, *A Bee in the Mouth: Anger in America Now* (New York: Encounter Books, 2006).

5. Cited by *GQ Magazine*, June 1999, 251; see also http://www.emophilips.com.

6. This section also appears in White, *Christ Among the Dragons*, 102–5.

7. David Aikman, "Attack Dogs of Christendom," *Christianity Today*, August 2007, 52.

8. On this, see the author's *Rethinking the Church* (Grand Rapids: Baker, 2003).

9. Cited by William Martin, *A Prophet with Honor: The Billy Graham Story* (New York: William Morrow, 1991), 318.

10. Francis Schaeffer, *The Great Evangelical Disaster* (Wheaton: Crossway, 1984), 174.

11. Much of this section is taken from White, *Christ Among the Dragons*, 105–8.

12. Michael Green, *Evangelism in the Early Church* (Grand Rapids: Eerdmans, 2003).

13. From the *Apology of Tertullian*, AD 197.

14. Francis Schaeffer, *Mark of the Christian* (Downers Grove, IL: InterVarsity, 1976), 151.

15. The following discussion of Lovemarks also appears in White, *Christ Among the Dragons*, 108–9.

16. See http://www.lovemarks.com; Kevin Roberts, *Lovemarks: The Future Beyond Brands* (Brooklyn, NY: PowerHouse Books, 2004), and *The Lovemarks Effect: Winning in the Consumer Revolution* (Brooklyn, NY: PowerHouse Books, 2006).

17. Schaeffer, *Mark of the Christian*, 161.

18. Ibid.

Chapter 12 Opening the Front Door

1. Some of the illustrations in this chapter are adapted from chapter 5 of my book *What They Didn't Teach You in Seminary* (Grand Rapids: Baker, 2011), 45–52.

2. Thom S. Rainer, *The Unchurched Next Door: Understanding Faith Stages* (Grand Rapids: Zondervan, 2003).

3. 1985 Technical Assistance Research Program (TARP) study for the White House Office of Consumer Affairs, 1985.

4. 1988 Technical Assistance Research Program (TARP) study for the White House Office of Consumer Affairs. The actual results regarding why customers did not return to a particular establishment were as follows: 1 percent died, 3 percent moved, 5 percent due to friendship, 9 percent due to competition, 14 percent as a result of product dissatisfaction, and 68 percent as a result of an indifferent, unfriendly employee attitude.

5. Ross Rankin, "Survey: Many at Church Not Helping Others Grow," *Baptist Press*, April 25, 2013, http://www.bpnews.net/BPnews.asp?ID=40152.

6. *Sister Act*, written by Joseph Howard and directed by Emile Ardolino, Touchstone Pictures, 1992.

7. For more on this, see the author's *Rethinking the Church*.

8. James Belasco, *Teaching the Elephant to Dance: Empowering Change in Your Organization* (New York: Crown Publishers, 1990), 213.

9. Ibid., 14.

10. Flavia Di Consiglio, "Lindisfarne Gospels: Why Is This Book So Special?" *BBC Religion and Ethics*, March 20, 2013, http://www.bbc.co.uk/religion/0/21588667.

11. James Emery White, *Church in an Age of Crisis* (Grand Rapids, MI: Baker, 2010).

12. Umberto Eco, *Travels in Hyper Reality: Essays*, trans. William Weaver (San Diego: Harcourt Brace Jovanovich, 1986), 73.

Chapter 13 Reimagining the Church

1. I have made similar arguments to what follows in various places, such as *Serious Times*, *Christ Among the Dragons*, and *Church in an Age of Crisis*.

2. Berger, "The Desecularization of the World: A Global Overview," in *Desecularization of the World*, ed. Berger, 4.

3. Lesslie Newbigin, *The Gospel in a Pluralist Society* (Grand Rapids, MI: Eerdmans, 1989), 227.

4. Bruce, *God Is Dead*, 148.

5. These words are affirmed in both the Nicene Creed (AD 325) and the Niceno-Constantinopolitan Creed (AD 381). Much of this section also appears in White, *Christ Among the Dragons*, 146–47.

6. John Calvin, *Institutes* 4.1.9.

7. Carl F. Henry, *God, Revelation and Authority* (Wheaton: Crossway, 1999).

8. As described by Wesley K. Willmer, J. David Schmidt, and Martyn Smith, *The Prospering Parachurch: Enlarging the Boundaries of God's Kingdom* (San Francisco: Jossey-Bass, 1998), xii.

9. The idea of the Holy Spirit as *paracletos* is first mentioned in John 14. For background on the meaning of the term, see the article "Advocate, Paraclete, Helper" (*parakletos*) in *New International Dictionary of New Testament Theology* 1, ed. Colin Brown (Grand Rapids, MI: Regency, 1975; repr., Grand Rapids, MI: Zondervan, 1986), 88–92.

10. Willmer, Schmidt, and Smith, *Prospering Parachurch*, xiv.

11. D. Michael Lindsay, "A Gated Community in the Evangelical World," *USA Today*, February 11, 2008, 13A.

12. Philip D. Kenneson, "There's No Such Thing as Objective Truth, and It's a Good Thing, Too" in *Christian Apologetics in the Postmodern World*, ed. Timothy R. Phillips and Dennis L. Okholm (Downers Grove, IL: InterVarsity, 1995), 162.

13. Much of this section also appears in White, *Christ Among the Dragons*, 158–9.

14. Katie Galli, "Dear Disillusioned Generation," *Christianity Today*, April 21, 2008, http://www.christianitytoday.com/ct/2008/april/28.69.html.

15. Ibid.

16. Philip Yancey, *Church: Why Bother? My Personal Pilgrimage* (Grand Rapids, MI: Zondervan, 1998), 23.

17. Sarah Cunningham, *Dear Church: Letters from a Disillusioned Generation* (Grand Rapids, MI: Zondervan, 2006), 13.

18. Ibid., 42.

19. Jürgen Moltmann, *The Church in the Power of the Spirit* (New York: Harper and Row, 1977), 10. See also Darrell L. Guder, ed., *Missional Church: A Vision for the Sending of the Church in North America* (Grand Rapids, MI: Eerdmans, 1998).

20. Christopher J. H. Wright, *The Mission of God: Unlocking the Bible's Grand Narrative* (Downers Grove, IL: InterVarsity, 2006), 22–23.

21. Adapted from Hybels, *Courageous Leadership* (Grand Rapids: Zondervan, 2002), 18–21.

22. Ibid., 21.

23. Newbigin, *Gospel in a Pluralist Society*, 227.

Afterword

1. Roger Finke and Rodney Stark, *The Churching of America 1776–1990* (New Brunswick, NJ: Rutgers University Press, 1992), 1.

Appendix A

1. Philip Yancey, *The Jesus I Never Knew* (Grand Rapids, MI: Zondervan, 2002), 147–48.

2. John Stott, *The Message of the Sermon on the Mount* (Downers Grove, IL: InterVarsity Press, 1978), 176.

3. Will D. Campbell, *Brother to a Dragonfly* (New York: Continuum, 1987), 220.

4. Uncommon Church, "Become Uncommon: A Welcome Letter," http://uncommon austin.com/become-uncommon.

Appendix B

1. Friedrich Nietzsche's famed "God is dead" passage can be found in section 125 of *The Gay Science*, in *The Portable Nietzsche*, ed. Walter Kaufmann (New York: Penguin, 1982), 95–96.

2. Falsani, "The Trouble with Labels."

3. Hiatt, "Marcus Mumford."

James Emery White, PhD, is the founding and senior pastor of Mecklenburg Community Church in Charlotte, North Carolina. He is also the president of Serious Times, a ministry that explores the intersection of faith and culture. He is ranked adjunctive professor of theology and culture of Gordon-Conwell Theological Seminary and also served as their fourth president. He is the author of nearly twenty books that have been translated into ten languages. You can read his blog at www.churchandculture.org and follow him on Twitter @JamesEmeryWhite.

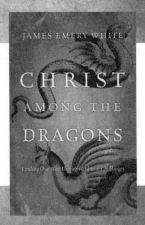